what grows

nine expressions

love
joy
peace
forbearance
kindness
goodness
faithfulness
gentleness
self-control

curated by: paul asjes

Yellow Suit Publishing
Ankeny, Iowa

what grows

First Edition: December 2025

Cover Photo: Katrina Hawthorne
Illustrations and Interior Photos: Chad Michael Cox

Published by Yellow Suit Publishing
Ankeny, Iowa

www.yellowsuitpublishing.com

ISBN 978-1-7356718-7-1

The quality of fruit that a plant produces depends on its roots. This collection is dedicated to the people who have supported the development of my spiritual foundations. Thank you, Mom and Dad, for your intentionality and drive to help me establish strong values, and for modeling courage and growth. Thank you, Katy, for being such an inspiration for me in so many ways. Thank you, Bill, Ann, Clint, Kyle, and Luke Hawthorne, for helping me establish a firm foundation. Thank you, Burney Nadler, for your invaluable guidance at key moments in my life. Thank you, Iván, for being such a joyful and substantive person in my life. Thank you, Alfonso, for your partnership and wisdom. I am grateful for your presence in my life. Thank you, Chad, for believing in the power of our stories and for your patience. You all incarnate the love, joy, peace, patience, kindness, goodness, faithfulness, gentleness, and self-control that I desire to embody.

Paul Asjes
November 2025

self-control

by: greg francis

Greg Francis, hailing from the vibrant streets of Brooklyn, New York, emerged from a bustling household of seven siblings where finding his voice was as challenging as navigating a bustling city block. It was through his passion for storytelling that he discovered the freedom to let characters roam as they pleased, a journey that led him to self-publish a fiction novel and embark on his next literary adventure. When he's not crafting compelling narratives, Greg indulges in nostalgic trips through all things 90s and 2000s, finding inspiration in the cultural tapestry of those iconic decades.

I'm not even supposed to be here—like, where we are now. I come from the Beyond, which is way better than the Below, I hear. There have been quite a few debates about which of the two are better or even exist, but those are stories for another time. I want to tell you about how tomorrow will be my best birthday ever.

Before I ever had a birthday, or even lived on Earth, I lived in the Beyond where things were perfect. The only thing is, the Beyond didn't seem perfect until now. In fact, there's no place I'd rather be than back there with the people I love, in the place where rivers don't flow from eyes, and hearts don't feel hunger. I think that's a good way to put it.

There was chaos in the Beyond the last time I was there. That was decades ago, though. Many of the people, including those that I love, participated in the great rebellion. People didn't believe that the Directors were telling the truth about the Sun, Moon, and stars. Mostly, people had doubts about Earth. They did not believe that it was impure, and included things like pain or sacrifice, no matter how much the Directors insisted. And so the trials were created.

Among the many different names, I could easily hear mine as people called out to their loved ones. No one wanted anyone they knew to do the trials. "Sebastian! What if you never make it back?" My mother did not doubt the Directors. I assured her that I had not doubted them either, I simply needed a faith of my own. Besides, the others that had gone before me and made it back spoke of indescribable truths. These truths did not counter what the Directors said— they simply included stories that did not exist in the Beyond. Those who returned from Earth spoke of things like passion, angst, rage, and infatuation. These words and the feelings they were tethered to were all so foreign to the people that called the Beyond home. By this, I was convinced to see for myself.

Due to some merit performed in a time that I cannot remember, I earned my citizenship in the Beyond, narrowly escaping an eternity in the Below. The Directors made a point to remind me of that part. And since there was no risk of ever being sent to the Below, my only risk was arriving on Earth and finding that the others before me had lied.

I remember the look on my mother's face before I entered the pod. I remember the THUD as I landed on Earth, instantly forgetting all that there is to know about anything. And at age 4, on a cold floor in an apartment on the Lower East Side of Manhattan, I became conscious of the Below, the Beyond, the decision I made to come and see for myself. Most importantly, I remember the rules.

The rules were what came to me most clearly. Not because I have some great hold on what it means to be moral or upright—quite the contrary, in fact. The Directors made it very clear that the reason I'm stuck on Earth is because of my lack of morality and civility. I guess those are my words, not theirs. Instead, they actually supposed that I had been lacking self-control.

That's right. It turns out that although there is no threat of being sent to The Below, I somehow have lost hold of the qualities that got me into The Beyond in the first place. Hardly worth my time here on Earth, if you ask me. Without the qualities that it takes to enter the Beyond again, I'm stuck here on Earth. Stuck until I get them back. Stuck here with rage, and passion. Stuck, every birthday.

I have learned things that the ones that came here before me left out of their stories when they returned. Like what it means to feel like a part of you is somewhere else. Surely, I feel like all of my happiness and all of my safety is in the Beyond with my mother. The mother I have been given on Earth is fine, I suppose. But nothing compares to the Beyond.

With every breaking of the Sun, accompanied by the sweet song of summer birds, I'm reminded that it has been almost thirty-six summers since I volunteered to come here. Every birthday has been an oxymoronic reminder that I still could not master what I'd been sent here for. In all that I've experienced here, I can't get my hands on self-control.

The rules we were given are simple, really. 1. Tell no one about the Beyond and 2. Live everyday like it is the last. That's it. We were free to live a life on Earth that might answer all of our questions, so long as we followed these two rules. At first, I thought it was rule number one that would keep me from home for so long. It wasn't until now that I realized that it was actually rule number two that had been driving self-control further and further from my grasp.

As I lay here, having lost everything, I'm fairly certain that tonight is the night that I leave this planet and return to the Beyond for good. I'm so certain, in fact, that I guess now is as good a time as any to tell you exactly how I figured it out.

I certainly did not know self-control at age six. I mean, which of us did? I hardly grasped the idea at that age and it was no surprise to my Aunt

Sandy. After all, it was her who'd found me hunched over beneath my school homework bench. It was a plastic kiddie table made up of vibrant blues, yellows and reds; and I, a dull brown as I lay there, hoping to vomit the twelve coffee cakes I'd downed just minutes before Aunt Sandy discovered the troubling scene. When asked why I was feeling so sick all of a sudden, I boasted through the pain that I simply wanted "coffee breath" the way my first grade teacher, Ms. Lewis, had sported each morning. It was the smell of her morning brew that escaped her mouth and snagged onto her perfume before it made its way over my shoulder when she was close in her instruction to me. I thought that my determination to acquire the sweet smell for myself at home would be seen as admirable, or smart, in the very least.

Aunt Sandy scolded me gently, making it a point to mention that I should have shown more self-control.

Surely, you'd think I'd figured it out an entire decade after the coffee cake fiasco, but no. Even at sixteen years old I found that I had still been lacking self-control. By now, even the Directors had begun to show a certain degree of concern for my lack of development in this particular area. Kindness, gentleness, joy—no problem. I exercised them with ease. But for some reason, I just could not get self-control well—under control.

"None of the others have shown an apprehension the way he has," they discussed among one another as if I were not present. I could tell that their patience had been strained and I was quickly running out of time. Nevertheless, the Directors allowed me to begin my junior year of high school. And I, accompanied by my optimistic bliss, was certain that I would finally figure it out once and for all.

In my sixteenth year here, I met Lori Washington. And while I knew the rules about love, its expressions and most notably—the rule about not telling anyone about the Beyond, Lori was an unmistakable challenge that kept me from being able to return to the Beyond. No doubt, she was of no help. We fell in love. We fell harder than I fell to this place almost thirty-six birthdays ago.

Falling in love was not against any of the rules. Even the Directors understood that it was uncontrollable and inevitable for even the strongest of us. However, they warned us extensively about the path that had been deemed 'certain.' It was the path that began at infatuation and made its final stop at the disclosure of the Beyond and all it entailed to people who could hardly understand it. We were not allowed to speak of it. I had heard many tales of the ones the went before me and thought themselves stronger. Each of them fell to the predicted fate. They found themselves smitten, and soon after, overly trusting, resulting in the untamed urge to tell their beloved about why they were on Earth, what they were sent to accomplish and what it meant to enter the Beyond after our trials. It was a troublesome matter that inundated the Directors each time they had to resolve the issue. It required tedious things like tying up loose ends and wiping the memories of those affected. Not impossible work, but a headache, without a doubt.

Even with this knowledge, I found myself without sobriety, neither emotionally or physiologically. It was irresponsible of me to think that skipping school with a teenage girl was conducive to me reaching my goal. In my defense, it was my first time on Earth and I just had to know if the stories were true. Was it true that there were bottles that contained boldness in the form of bitter fluids? Was it possible that the joy given by the joining of two minds could only be superseded by the union of consenting lips?

It was true. Every detail had not disappointed, except that it did not describe these things accurately enough. The stories I had heard completely lacked the explanation of these feelings in their totality. My love for Lori Washington was deep, wild and reciprocated. But the things it caused me to do were unwise. I am still ashamed of the reckless abandon that became me. In the end, I told Lori all there was to know about gods and goodness. I told her of evil and eternity. I spilled about the Beyond and about the Below. Even with all I had gained from loving her, I once again lost sight of self-control. In fact, it had never been further from me than at sixteen.

The Directors met with me recently. An entire twenty years after the Lori Washington fiasco. They had undoubtedly found themselves nearing the end of their grace with my trial. Most others had concluded their trials in a mere fraction of the time I had been taking. Somehow, I just could not get it right. Not when I was six, not at sixteen, not at twenty-six (the year I used frontal lobe development as an argument for an extension), but thirty-six would be different, I am sure. The Directors said all the things I knew they would. The data shows this and my trends have revealed that. See, but I've cracked the code.

In all my years, I loathed the candles and cake. Failure after failure, I could not understand how self-control had escaped me, even when I was sure that it could not be closer. Until I figured it out. Tomorrow is my thirty-sixth year here and if I have it my way, it will be my last. When I wake up tomorrow, the Directors will greet me and I will boast in my newfound wisdom. Actually, it'd be wise of them to get my living quarters ready. The Beyond is closer than ever. I declare that today will be my last.

Yesterday, I was thinking about how I even got here and that is how I figured out how to get home. I did not work or strive to get here. How silly of me to think that it would be part of how to return home. All these years, I've been on Earth pining and yearning for what is so freely given in the Beyond.

It's the meaning behind rule number 2.

I have not been living everyday like my last. Instead, I've spent years being controlled by the pursuit of something I already have access to. Today, I know exactly how to get it. For I am now certain that self-control is not found or lost. It is not fleeting, demanding that we pursue it with despair. No, I'm willing to bet that in order to have the control that I seek so badly, I need only ask. It's exactly what I'll wish for when I blow out my candles with the Directors tomorrow.

self-control

peace

by: cornelia asjes

Cornelia Asjes is a writer and nanny. Her poetry won the 2023 Colonel Darren L. Wright Award in Poetry, and has also been featured in Moonstone Arts Center's *The Weight of Motherhood*. Her fiction is forthcoming at Belletrist 7 Magazine. She lives in Kansas City, where she studies Creative Writing, MFA at the University of Missouri.

The Jersey kicked me in the face this morning. Nearly broke my jaw. I'm sure if I could look in a mirror I'd have a two-inch C-shaped gash cupping my under-eye. It's left me lying on the barn floor with a tremendous pain in my head for the past half-hour. I'll get up soon, maybe, or maybe lie here a bit longer. Nobody will come to find me for hours, maybe days with this snow.

Moments like these convince me that there is no karmic god. I did everything right this morning and still got walloped. I did not decide, in my half-sleep, to sell the farm for an extra fifteen minutes of rest. I didn't even look over to the empty spot in bed, where James used to lay next to me. About an hour ago, rising with the alarm, I planted my feet on the rag-rug. I switched on the yellow bedside light. I breathed in through my nose, out through my mouth, and calmly dressed myself against the cold. I took in every object that I could sense and left the non-sensible things to yesterday.

But even in the sensible world, I noticed my socks were growing thinner. My accounts ebb and no longer flow. My sister Ann incessantly goads me, "Sell the farm, Emily. Come live in the guest room." Her guest room in Brunswick has two twin beds with quilts we made as preteens in home-economics when we had no business dreaming of adult topics like the future. I think we wanted kitchens and families almost as soon as we clapped eyes on our mother. Our mother had enough hips and aprons and cast-iron skillets to inspire a generation of mothers, but we absorbed and kept it all to ourselves. In Ann's guest room I could wrap myself in my own youth every night, but I am sixty-two and with little to show for it in my own character beyond a stern resolve to punish myself. That, perhaps, is what the Jersey thinks.

I should've expected disaster. I should've seen it coming when the day started with negative twenty-five-degree wind chills. An unseasonable first blizzard of the year. This would've been James's day to milk the cow, and I'd have stayed in. Sparked the kettle. Brewed an English Breakfast and cozied into the big leather chair, James's chair by the window, to watch the sun rise through a veil of flurries. I would have cooked breakfast if he were here. If I slept in today, though, the Jersey's teats would have been sore in an hour, hard in three, and impacted beyond my skill to repair by the time the sun warmed the sting out of the wind.

The fact is, she's twelve, the cow, and having trouble coping with age. I see myself in her sometimes. And I see James. He bought me her grandmother more than thirty years ago, and we birthed two more generations of Jerseys from that first heifer, together, in this very barn. Each time, James had to reach elbow-deep into the heifer and help a slick purple calf out. I have seen a purple cow. I've seen two little purple cows transform into velvet, doe-eyed, gangly things. I've seen this small zone of the Hudson Valley kept on illegal raw milk for decades, and not a soul has perished from it. To be a cow and feed the world. I will be one in another life.

Enough light has come in now that I can see the Jersey's big soft slick nose. In the confusion of my fall after she kicked me, the electric lantern fell and went out. We don't have electricity to the barn yet, but we were considering it before James's heart attack. Her nose is right above mine, suspended with mild disinterest in the fact that I'm lying here, not milking her. I was almost done anyway.

This cow. She brought trouble from the start, killing her own mother during birth. She was born, right in this barn-stall, in a snowstorm much like this one. A prolapsed uterus made the occasion tricky at best, and although she came out fine with James's help, the vet couldn't make it in time to stop the bleeding and clear the infection, and the old heifer, her mother, died four days later. We did our best, but it was her time. I bottle-fed this Jersey from her first week of life. And now she kicks me.

Maybe this Jersey was mad at me for never gifting her children. We bred her from the previous two generations, but she was going to be our last one. Maybe we stifled her chance at eternal return.

I read in Plato that love, even erotic love, is our yearning for eternity. We cannot live forever but through children. James and I deprived this Jersey of eternity. Perhaps she is bitter, although I doubt cows are capable of bitterness.

Someone once said that at the beginning of time, orb-like creatures roamed the earth contentedly until they were unhappily cut in half by the gods. To this day, men and women, incomplete half-orbs, still wander far and wide, seeking out their other halves, driven by loneliness and longing for the complete orb. This is a mythology I can get behind. It rings true. It is a hard thing, though, when your other hemisphere vanishes completely. There is nowhere I can wander, nowhere in upstate New York, nor the United States, nor beyond, to find James. He is only here, and only in memory. I should tell Ann the real reason I will never leave the farm. It's ground zero for my attempt at eternity. This is where James and I tried to live forever.

One of the first things we learned about each other when we met was that we wanted lots of kids. As children, we both read Robert Frost's You Come Too and wanted to read his poetry to our own kids someday. The verses took on a new emotion after we lost a first and then a second baby—the waste of hopes and of life, so crushing, came as easily as blowing leaves.

I'm going out to fetch the little calf
That's standing by the mother. It's so young,
It totters when she licks it with her tongue.
I sha'n't be gone long —you come too.

James read it to me and we consoled each other with our own cows and calves thirty years ago. He told me we had each other. We'd have a cow and a little calf too. Such a delicate thing, infancy.

Many wonder how a good god could exist alongside all the suffering in this universe, but I look at things differently. How could the same force that brings in miscarriages and wind-chills and heart attacks also invent the soft ears of a calf, or springy turf in April after a winter of death, or leather-like hands to hold your own when you're postpartum and hurting. I don't believe in a cruel god, but a fickle one. Fickle like me. Fickle like this Jersey, calmly chewing her cud after she undoubtedly caused my brain to bleed. God-as-cow.

I have better things to wonder about than the problem of pain. Pain comes easy, but choices do not. I often wonder if we made the right decision, never trying for kids again after the first two. Not adopting. At the time it seemed too great a risk. The loss of the first child had nearly turned us to stone. The second had shattered us. What would another do?

Ann has little to offer her children. I love my nieces and nephews, but they suffer so little, and I can't help but look down on them for it. I like to think I would've had my boy or my girl out early to milk or shovel snow before school. I like to think they would've hated the work, but then come to appreciate it later in life. I still believe in something like character. In being good. In bringing beauty into the world through pain. Maybe that's all I believe in, come to think of it.

Now, though, when you encourage kids to work with their hands, to skip the desk job, to go against the grain, you're asking them to be poor, or at least unstable. You're depriving them of a future. Of being able to have their own kids. Of their own eternal return. Ann's kids are set up to both be accountants. They will be comfortable for the rest of their lives. I would be a fool not to give my kids the same option of comfort. They would be fools not to take it. Corporate farms ate up James's beloved land. They are the enemy. My kids would most likely end up working for the enemy. That's what the farm kids in the area do these days.

So, I'm fickle as to whether we should've had kids. Whether I would've been a good mother. Whatever a good mother is in this world.

I have waffled on whether it was the right decision, but a few weeks ago, James went into cardiac arrest, and he was gone in an hour. Now I know I only ever had three great losses in me. I still can't seem to wrap my mind around his lingering presence. You expect absence after death, but every object points its way down to the dead, and in this way, James has been with me more than ever recently. The barn rafters above me are already cobwebbed, for instance, and he's only been gone a few weeks. He never would have let that happen. When he died, I prayed that I'd get a sudden one, too.

The rafters are cobwebbed. The driveway is unplowed, and underneath the snow the leaves piled up. Last week, Bud came over from next door (next door being a mile west) and did the milking, brought me enough dinner to weather the longest winter. I stayed in bed mostly, feeling sorry for myself. I don't really believe in an afterlife, you see. But I feel weak and stupid for hoping in one now that someone I love is gone. It's one thing to prove logically that god is dead. It's another thing entirely to live with the consequences in your heart when you see your loved one fade off into nothing. Not into heaven. I grappled a lot with that last week, but just now, I think I've arrived at some form of consolation.

James is here on the farm. We are here together, whatever exists of our realities and our dreams. Even the memories of winter mornings and negative twenty-five degrees, of miscarriages, of coming out to discover dead heifers, somehow they crowd out the reality of upstate New York or the memories of my childhood, of my mother. In retrospect, life didn't mean much to me before James, except that it pointed toward him. Of course, I'll never move in with Ann. Never move away from here.

Mother always told us to find someone who loved us more than we loved ourselves, who lived life better than we did, and who had more fun than anyone at the party. She instilled in us a standard so high that Ann ignored it entirely and married a rich little boring accountant, and stayed close to home, and I never found anyone good enough to fit the bill. I never found anyone, at least, in my mother's lifetime. By the time she passed, she thought I was a dried-up old maid at twenty-nine.

When I finally found James (in the year of my mother's death), he fit the bill. I doubted that mother was looking down from a cloud, but her existence, perched on the kitchen counter of my own memories, nodded approval. He used to recite poetry to me.

Till a' the seas gang dry, my dear
And the rocks melt wi' the sun;
I will love thee still, my dear,
While the sands o' life shall run.

He gave me a corny, eternal kind of love. One I'd never considered for myself.

I think I was good for him, too. He had to sell his forty-head of cows once New York State Ordinances drove out the smaller farm-collectives. Ironically, only the rich can become hobby farmers now. It was hard for James to give up the farm, and then lose two children. It was hard for him, but I was always weaker. I can't be sure, but I think I loved him more. I needed him more than he needed me.

We met under this very barn ceiling. He was much older. I was in overalls, auditing tuberculin testing for smaller Hudson Valley livestock operations—the rare woman in the field. We discussed impending changes in the federal code that would edge out his small operation. He was privately raising forty grass-fed beef steers per year when we met.

"You're going to need a helluva lot more than forty-head to keep floating by this time next year," I'd said.

"Can I buy you dinner?" He asked.

Would it be strange to say that I already loved him?

I'm going now, I think. I don't care if there's no heaven, and only nothing. The losses in my life proved one thing, and more clearly than a shooting star, more obvious than a winter dawn on fresh snow: having must be worth something if losing is so damned painful. I guess that means that my life has been worth something. Enough. In the end, life itself will be one of the easier things I've given up. Leaving it will be like tossing out these worn old socks. I'm sure it's growing lighter outside, but I can barely see anything now.

One of my favorite memories has no image. I was blindfolded. It was springtime, a Sunday after church. I had spent the muddy season walking around with a scabbed wound in my heart and a vacancy in my womb, but it was finally sunny. I was wearing a green poplin dress, and James was in his shirtsleeves. James had taken the scarf out of my hair and tied it around my eyes and spun me around. He led me by the hand, every now and then guiding my shoulder through the screen door, or past the watering spigot. I remember the soft grass under my heels and toes. The poking gravel of the farm-lot. I remember laughing, a rare gift in that season of my life. He slowed me down. I felt the transition from sunshine to barn-cool.

"Are you ready for this?"

He took my hand and set it on the warm flank of a Jersey cow. He whipped off the scarf. My feet were standing in the very spot in the barn where the small of my back rests at this moment. A new and warm life has always been by me, thanks to James.

I can't even feel the pain in my head anymore. I think I'll sleep. For a long time, I'll sleep.

peace

gentleness

by: breanna rae

Breanna Rae fell down the rabbit hole at the youngest of a grand age, and she has spent her time composing, dancing, painting, sewing, and reciting odd things about crocodiles ever since. She writes poetry when she isn't otherwise occupied, and prefers to not write such nonsense when she is, in fact, quite occupied. Her artwork first displayed inside the halls of a real castle, because of course, and she has studied the great poets of lore including Poe, Plath, and Alice by way of Carroll.

What if I feel

like a phantom caught
under the weight of the toll-
ing bell that rings away time
as I hope to become
part of the lore of the human race
but go on with expression so wan
to listen
to those who are languid-
ly singing the song
or the dirge of all that is civil
I fall-
ing down into torpor
I'm trying to call
for anything good and tru-
thfully failing to find
the answers I need through the
glare of it all
I expect-
ations that I never stall
I expect-
ing an end to the wrong
I search for the meaning
of gallantly strong

Guess I didn't know
that could take so long

gentleness

forbearance

by: paul asjes

Paul Asjes was born and raised in Des Moines, Iowa. He spent many summers gardening in Stillwater, Minnesota, and canoeing in the Boundary Waters. He is currently a New York City educator. He has taught math, art, history, reading, and writing. After Colin Witt trained him for his first marathon over a decade ago, Paul loves running. Paul believes that habits help determine our destiny. His book Isaiah's First Winter is a 2023 Mom's Choice Awards® GOLD Award winner.

The town of Stillwater lay cradled in a bend in the river, its streets winding like the worn, sometimes cracked, coils of an old, weathered bracelet. The schoolhouse, built by the community years ago, with its strange, symmetrical beauty, seemed to breathe in time with the seasons. Its windows glimmered like the river's surface. The building was not just a place of learning, it was alive, infused with the very spirit of the town. Ivy clung to the stone walls as if it too had a purpose here, its leaves whispering bits of wisdom to the wind. Inside, the wood was warm and dark, and the air hummed with the gentle pulse of time itself, stretching endlessly in a way that was comforting. Everything in the nursery, the books, the fabrics, the hand-drawn pictures of imagined futures, was imbued with a quiet magic. Every detail was intentionally designed to nurture the children, to keep them safe until they discovered the one thing that would release them from the nursery's walls.

Beyond the schoolhouse, Stillwater unfurled like a well-worn quilt, each street revealing neighborhoods that teamed with life. Gardens spilled over mossy stone walls, their blooms reaching out knowingly to each passersby. Both the gardeners and their gardens were the secret guardians of the town's quiet peace. The roses, impossibly vibrant, drew their strength from the ritual offerings buried beneath their roots: fish carcasses laid to rest after each filleting, their decomposing bodies feeding the soil until beauty emerged from decay. The bakeries scented the air with hints of cinnamon and vanilla that drifted through the town square, where the fountain flowed steadily throughout the day. Children who had completed their Discoveries could be seen walking purposefully through town, their newfound confidence visible in the set of their shoulders. The whole community existed in a delicate harmony, like notes unfolding in a complex melody. Each person contributed their unique gift to the symphony of daily life, while the river that gave the town its name gurgled in harmony with the sounds of Stillwater's inhabitants.

But for Evan, the thing that would set him free had eluded him for longer than he wanted. Month after month, the other children—his friends, his companions—were released from the school, their faces bright with the gleam of something new, something they had created. They moved on to take their place in the world. A word, a thought, a shape that had never existed before. Some of them invented new words as easily as breathing, their voices spilling them into the world like droplets from a clear spring. They left the nursery with the grace of birds taking flight, their futures spread out before them like a clear, open sky. Others, like Theo, fumbled at first, stumbling over syllables and meanings, but eventually, they too found their Discovery. Evan, however, felt as though he was standing on the edge of a great expanse, gazing into the unknown. His Discovery hovered before him, just beyond his reach, a shadow that danced and shifted as he stretched out his hand. Sometimes, when the teacher's back was turned, Evan could have sworn the walls whispered, "Don't worry, Evan. We're just waiting for the perfect moment... Any second now..."

When the school celebrated, Evan smiled and celebrated too. But it was becoming harder and harder for Evan to summon a genuine smile. Evan watched, helpless, as his friends discovered their gifts, one by one. Each new word, each new idea that bloomed in their minds seemed to highlight a hollow space in his own. And today, it was Kieran. Kieran had been a quiet one, almost as reserved as Evan, but today, when he stood in front of the class, his voice clear and steady, he had discovered a word that had made them all sit up and listen. A word that seemed to shimmer in the air, different from the rest, as though it had come from somewhere far beyond the walls of the nursery. The moment had passed rather quickly, but Evan had seen it, the way Kieran's face lit up with that look, the look that he knew so well. It was the look of discovery. His face showed evidence that something had irreversibly changed, something he could never unlearn. And now, as Kieran stood before the group, smiling with the same quiet grace, Evan found himself staring at him, knowing that in just a moment, he would leave. He would step out of the school and into the world. Without him. "Goodbye, Evan," he said, his voice soft, but not sad. "Goodbye."

Evan's struggle was not his alone. The heft of his parents' unspoken expectations weighed heavily on him, far more than he could even admit to himself. At night on the weekends he was home, he'd sometimes hear their hushed voices through the walls, discussing how much longer it might take for him to find his Skill. His mother, usually so gentle, would sigh and look at him with an expression that was a mixture of concern and frustration, as if waiting for him to unlock the secret of his own potential. His father, more silent than usual, would only shake his head and mutter that, "some children take longer to find their way."The words were heavy, as if he too were growing impatient, weights Evan could feel pressing on his shoulders. Even at the dinner table, their conversations always seemed to circle back to the nursery. His father would ask, "I wonder what Evan's Discovery will be?" Though Evan could hear the hint of doubt in his voice. "Soon, surely, soon."

Evan lay in bed, not quite dreaming, not awake. He mulled over the last few students who had left. He analyzed every interaction he had with them. He remembered their moments of discovery, their faces lighting up, their families beaming with pride when they came. What was it like to know, to feel the moment when your Skill was finally revealed? He closed his eyes and saw their faces again, some laughing, some crying, their gifts as natural as breathing. The air around them seemed to hum with certainty, a certainty that he could never quite grasp. For Evan, it was as though the world itself was a puzzle with pieces he couldn't quite fit together. And yet, no matter how many times he tried to make sense of it, the answer remained elusive, just beyond his reach. He wondered if they ever felt the way he did. He truly felt like the last person in a race everyone else had already finished. And in that quiet, restless space between sleep and wakefulness, he felt the weight of it all grow heavier still, pressing not just on his shoulders, but deep into the core of who he was. What if he never discovered his Skill at all? He was by far the tallest student in the school, and he was starting to feel an awkwardness to every moment. He realized he was beginning to avoid eye contact with his peers.

As Evan looked around the school, it was not just a building. It was alive. Its walls pulsed with an unseen energy. The beams above, thick and gnarled with age, seemed to hum with a quiet song, and the floor beneath their feet was worn smooth, as though it too had been shaped by the endless shuffle of small feet. The lanterns that hung from the rafters burned not with mere flame, but with a fire that drew its warmth from the very heart of the earth. Due to these lanterns, at all hours of the day, the shadows on the walls moved as if alive, curling and stretching as the lights flickered. The scent of old paper mingled with the faint perfume of cedar drifting through the air. But despite all the comfort, the soft hum of the room, Evan felt no peace. It was his turn to work in the kitchen. As he kneaded the dough, he found himself daydreaming of life beyond the walls of the school. The space was thick with expectation. He often felt a silent force that pressed against him from all sides. Time here was strange, it flowed in ways that defied understanding. It was as though the very walls of the nursery had a memory of their own. It held the will of children long gone, their voices lingering in the corners, watching, waiting.

Every morning, the children would gather in the center of the room. They sat in a perfect circle, their legs crossed, their hands placed gently in their laps. Their eyes, wide and expectant, focused on the Teacher, a woman who was more presence than person. To the children she had no name, not truly; she was simply the Teacher, her essence intertwined with the very soul of the nursery. Her long, curly black ringlets of hair shimmered as they tumbled down her back. Some days her locks were braided into a pattern so intricate it seemed to pulse with meaning, other days it flowed freely. Evan sometimes got lost in her hair. Her eyes were pale and grey as marble, and when she looked at a child, it felt as though she was looking into their very core, seeing things you could not yet put into words. Her voice, when it came, was soft but carried the weight of age. When she spoke, it was not with a mere command but with the quiet authority of something that had always been and always would be.

"Today," she would announce, her voice cutting through the stillness, "we will practice the Skill." The words were never questioned. The Skill was as much a part of their world as the river that ran through the village, a river that curved and wound, offering its blessings in the form of small stones, smooth and glistening, for those who could find them. The Teacher's word was law, and the children knew they were here for one purpose: to find their place in the world, to speak their Truth into existence. The others seemed to understand instinctively. They worked in silence, their faces serene as if their thoughts were already taking shape before them. The air around them seemed to shimmer with the weight of their potential, as if they were becoming something greater with every passing moment. Some children used compasses to draw perfect arrangements of circles, others wrote poems with fine pens on beautiful tablets, still others chiseled away with tools.

But for Evan, each time the Teacher's words filled the room, the world seemed to grow smaller. The shadows in the corners deepened, curling closer around him like a thick fog, and a heaviness settled in his chest. He did not fear failure in the way others might. No. It was something far stranger. It was as if the Discovery itself had taken on a life of its own, something that did not belong to him, something that slipped through his fingers like water. He had tried, day after day, in secret and in public, to reach for it. He had spoken to the air, called out to the walls, but the words he needed never came. He had watched the others, seen their faces light up with recognition as they unlocked their Skill, but each time, his heart twisted with the fear that perhaps he was not meant for this at all. Perhaps a Discovery was not his to find.

One afternoon, as the other children worked through their motions, Evan found himself drawn to the window. His gaze drifted past the nursery walls, past the familiar streets of Stillwater, and out to the open fields beyond. The landscape was not as it seemed. The sky was alive, shifting in hues of gold and lavender, and the trees at the edge of the meadow moved as if they were stretching and yawning. He could hear the wind, but it was not the wind of this world. It was something deeper, something older, a sound that whispered of forgotten times. The birds that flitted across the sky were not birds at all, but shadows of creatures that had not existed for centuries, their wings beating with a rhythm that matched the pulse of the earth itself. For the briefest moment, Evan wondered again if the Discovery was not something to be found, but something to be created. Maybe it was something born of the very world around him.

Evan sat quietly, his gaze drifting toward the window once more. The familiar rhythm of the nursery had settled into a soft hum around him, but he felt a restlessness stirring deep inside. The Teacher's voice broke through the silence, but it didn't feel like a command. It was a soft murmur, distant, like the sound of a river far below. "Evan," she said, and her eyes met his with an intensity that seemed to burn right through him. "You have been quiet today." Her words were not a reprimand, not a judgment. They were simply a recognition, a statement. For a what felt like a very long moment, Evan froze, unsure how to respond. But then, something shifted within him, a small, tentative clarity. He spoke slowly, almost as if testing the words as they left his mouth. "I think… I think I've been waiting for something to happen. Waiting for my Skill to show up." He paused, feeling foolish as the words left him. The Teacher tilted her head slightly, her gaze never leaving his. She smiled gently, but it wasn't the smile of someone offering comfort. It was the smile of someone who knew exactly what was unfolding. "Evan," she said, her voice low, "sometimes, it's not about waiting. It's about seeing what is already there. You've been looking for your Skill as if it is something separate from you, something to be found. But perhaps it is something you are already becoming, something deep inside." Her words sank into him like a spring rain sinking into the earth. There was no sudden flash of understanding, no burst of light. But in that moment, he felt it, the quiet, undeniable shift. For the first time, the weight of his uncertainty felt less like a burden and more like an invitation. He wasn't waiting for something outside of him.

He was learning how to recognize what had always been there, right in front of him. The Teacher gave him one last, knowing look before turning away, but the impact of her words lingered in the space between them. And for the first time in a long while, Evan didn't feel so lost.

Weeks passed, and with each day, Evan found himself watching more closely, not just the other children but the small, unspoken movements of the world around him. One afternoon, he sat by the window, watching a younger student struggle with a puzzle. The boy's hands trembled as he fumbled with the pieces, frustration tightening his small face. Evan felt a tug in his chest, something raw and familiar. I've been there. His mind flashed to the countless times he had felt just as lost, his hands useless, his mind blank. He remembered the days when the pieces wouldn't fit, no matter how hard he tried to force them together. And then, without thinking, he pointed, just a simple gesture, nothing grand, no words of advice. The boy stopped, following his finger, and slowly, carefully, slid the final piece into place. The room seemed to hold its breath for a moment. Evan's heart skipped. That was it. That was *me*. His Skill wasn't about speaking or creating, not in the way he'd always imagined. It wasn't about making something new. It was about seeing what others couldn't. It was about understanding when to act, when to be still.

His hands felt light, his chest unburdened. The room around him didn't change, but he did. He had been looking for something grand, something that would shine and burst into the world. But his Discovery, his Skill, had always been there, quiet and steady, a part of him, like the river that wound through Stillwater, always moving, always connected to the land around it. Evan stood up, feeling the weight of his own presence in a way he never had before. The whole world hadn't opened in an instant, but in that moment, he felt the peace, and that was enough.

He smiled softly, watching the boy's face light up as he finally saw the puzzle come together. Evan hadn't done it for him, but he had helped him find his own way. And that was Evan's gift.

forbearance

goodness

by: joshua seidler

Joshua Seidler was born on the mission field of the Navajo Nation reservation where he has a faded memory of speaking Navajo as a toddler. He now lives in a small town in the Colorado Rocky Mountains where he spends as much time as possible breathing fresh air with his wife and children. Using his love of family and the outdoors, Joshua inspires readers to faith and imagination in his stories like the beloved *Pup Goes Home* and in his poetry collections that offer an imaginative twist on Shakespearean sonnets.

Dustin slapped the top of the steering wheel and growled, "Seriously?" as he slammed on the brakes. Eight intersections between his house and the parts store and he felt like he had caught all reds. He stared in a daze at the stoplight swaying on its line over the intersection and his brain went over the list of items he was supposed to buy.

Gasket, hose, hose clamps, oxygen sensor.

Three hundred dollars.

Back home in the garage that smelled like tires and grease, his dad had just stared at the parts store website. "Wow! These sensors only used to be 50 bucks".

Dustin was quiet, annoyed. He was broke and didn't get paid until next week. Somehow Dad knew that. As Dad pulled a bottle from the beer fridge he said, "You can borrow the money. I know you need your car for work. But I don't have a lot of time. You need to go buy the parts while I work on these rusted bolts." Dad hooked the beer under the bottle opener bolted to the workbench and popped the cap off. He took a sip and tossed his truck keys to Dustin.

Dustin failed to catch the keys and had to pick them off the ground, worsening a headache that had been brewing all day. In a huff he stomped toward the old truck. He was just about to grab the handle when his dad said, "Hey, hey, hey! Maybe clean up first?"

Dustin looked at his greasy hands then did a sharp turn and headed into the house to wash. He was annoyed. His friends didn't have to spend their time working on cars; they all had parents who could afford a real mechanic for their cars. And they all had nice cars. Dustin's was...not nice. It wasn't terrible; it was a Toyota that got good gas mileage and had never left him stranded. But it was 23 years old and it seemed like there was always something to work on: loose suspension, rattling interior, door that wouldn't lock, and now this dumb check engine light came on this morning. That had screwed up his whole day because Dad couldn't help him until he came home from work. He was always scared to work on his car without Dad, scared he would mess something up.

The street light turned green; Dustin floored his dad's old truck and swerved into the parking lot with a tire squeal. That earned a scowl from a skinny guy in sweat pants walking a French bulldog.

Inside the store, the parts kid said, "Year, make, and model?"

"My dad said I need Denso part #PS-23-6" Dustin answered. "It's an oxygen sensor".

"I need the year, make, and model," the kid repeated. He had no name tag but the thin mustache, flat-brim cap and energy drink in his hand made him look like a meme.

A short stare-down ensued between the kid and Dustin. Dustin was intimidated here; he knew a few things about cars but he didn't know enough. So he assumed that anyone who worked in an auto-parts store must know a lot about cars.

Finally, Dustin surrendered, "It's a Toyota Corolla. 2002."

The kid tapped some keys and then spun the monitor around so Dustin could see. "We have three options for your car. First one is $105 and comes with a one-year warranty. Store brand is $188 and comes with a three-year warranty. OEM part you asked for is $290 and doesn't say anything about the warranty."

Dustin brightened at the thought of a cheaper part. He asked, "Which one is the best?"

The kid shrugged as he grabbed a quick sip of energy drink. "We usually recommend the three-year warranty."

Dustin thought, "Of course you do. Store brand."

"Could I look at them?" Dustin asked meekly.

The kid nodded knowingly, disappeared behind some racks, and returned with three small boxes.

The OEM sensor was in a plain brown box, wrapped in a simple plastic bag; it was heavy and dull looking. The store brand sensor was in a green box with the store's logo plastered on every side. The cheap sensor was somehow much lighter than the other two; in a shiny silver box, it was wrapped in iridescent plastic and cradled by smooth black foam.

Dustin thought the cheap sensor looked just fine as he slid it back in the box. An image of his sun-burned Corolla was floating in his mind; he didn't want to keep it another year.

"You know what, I'll take this one" he said, pushing the more expensive parts across the counter.

The kid found the gasket, hose, and clamps Dustin needed and rang up the total. $111.89. Dustin actually grinned while paying for everything with some of the cash his dad had loaned him. He nearly floated all the way back to the truck.

Everything felt different as he drove home. He was making all the lights, his favorite song began to play on the radio, and he even laughed out loud when he saw the skinny guy in sweat pants picking up a dog turd with a pink baggie.

He glanced at the sun kissing the horizon and thought, "Sweet, I can still meet my friends for hot wings."

Inside the garage, his dad wasn't where he was supposed to be. He was standing at the workbench; blood was dripping from his hand.

Dustin stared awkwardly. His previous optimism began to sink into a sea of distraction.

"Sliced it deep," Dad simply said as he wrapped two band-aids around a bloody finger and then wiped the counter with a shop towel. He reached for his beer, took another sip, and eased onto a stool. Dustin eyed his dad to understand whether this was serious. Dad's hands were always dry, cut, and scarred. This appeared to be no different. Then Dustin remembered the extra $200 in his pocket and pulled out the bills and coins. He handed it back to his dad along with the bag of parts.

Dad was initially confused and then his eyebrow went up when he saw how much money was left. He briefly rummaged in the bag, then held up the shiny sensor box and said, "Not good."

"Huh?" Dustin asked.

Shaking his graying head, Dad said, "Why'd you buy this? It's the wrong part."

Defensively Dustin said, "Yeah it was cheaper. Way cheaper."

Dad stared hard at Dustin for the first time that afternoon. "It's cheaper for a reason. These Toyota's don't like generic parts, especially sensors and electronics. You have to get the real thing."

"I mean, the mechanic at the store said it would work. Can't we just try it? I was gonna go to the wing place tonight…" Dustin said desperately.

Dad rubbed his forehead, swirling blood into the dirt and grease. He said, "That wasn't a mechanic you talked to."

Dustin snapped back, "So? Who cares?"

Dad shook his head and said tersely, "Whatever. I'll regret this but let's do it."

Forty-five minutes later the car was back together. Dustin was in the driver's seat and his dad stood staring into the engine bay.

"OK, turn the key" Dad said. Dustin did.

The engine chuckled and chuckled but wouldn't catch.

Dad checked all the wire connections and then said, "Try it again."

Dustin said a silent half-prayer and turned the key again. Same result.

Right then Dustin's sister, Marcy, opened the door and said, "Mom said dinner's ready."

"Be right in," Dad responded. He grabbed a rag and began cleaning dirt off his hands. This caused one of the bandages to pull away.

Dustin panicked. He whined, "Dad, I wanted to go out! And I'll get fired if I don't get to work tomorrow!"

Dad's face reddened and he threw the rag onto the workbench rather harshly. As he walked out of the garage, he muttered, "Sorry bud, I don't know what to tell you. I have so much work to catch up on after dinner."

At the dinner table, Mom and Marcy were waiting patiently. Dad began to ease into his seat with a typical groan of weariness but Mom immediately noticed the blood and bandage on Dad's hand. "My goodness, Emmett, what happened?"

"It's fine," Dad said.

"It's not fine," she replied in her mom voice. "And you need to clean it better or it'll get infected! Now what did you do?"

In an annoyed voice, Dad said, "I let your son make a bad decision." He stood and ambled over to the old porcelain farmhouse sink where he ran water. He peeled the last bandage off and stuck his hands under the flow, just briefly; it brought a slight wince as the water ran pink. He shut the flow off and came back to the table with wet hands. Mom handed him a paper towel which he used to pat his hands dry.

Mom, confused, asked, "Dustin?"

Dad answered, "He got a bad part. A fake part."

Dustin should have known better but he couldn't keep his mouth shut. He didn't want Mom to think poorly of him. So, he protested, "Dad, it has a warranty!"

"Of course it does. They're selling you a warranty, not a working sensor'" Dad said, escalating his volume.

Mom said, "Emmett, take it easy on him..."

Dad shot her a glance and hasty words tumbled out, "Easy on him? He's got it easy. Me? I kill myself all day and then come home and have to work on his car. And is it nice father-son bonding time? No! He argues with me, does whatever he wants, and wastes time!"

The room was dead silent for many minutes. Marcy stared at Dad to see if he was going to yell again. Dusting quietly moved salad around his plate. And Mom's eyes were icicles, staring at Dad. Finally, Dad quietly said, "I'm sorry, Shirley."

Mom's eyes softened. Then she began to eat.

Dad turned back to Dustin. His voice was firm and final. "Do you know why I gave you the exact part number? So that you would get the exact part. The good one. The genuine one. But you let them sell you a cheap imitation, and it's no good. Your car still doesn't run and we've wasted time and money. Now we have to re-do everything. I don't know how you're getting to work tomorrow."

After dinner Dustin plopped onto the couch and clicked on a TV show. He was mad at himself; Dad was right. He usually was; Dad knew about these things...why hadn't he listened? Because that cheap, shiny sensor promised to be just as good.

Sometime around 10pm, Dad came into the living room smelling of oil and exhaust again and dropped Dustin's keys on the coffee table. He simply said, "There you go. Sorry for yelling." He walked away; a moment later the bath fan turned on and the shower began to spray.

Dustin walked over to the window and looked out on the dark street. His car was sitting neatly along the curb. While trying to understand, Dustin noticed his mom sitting at the table cradling a mug of tea in her small hands.

"He went back," she stated softly. "He actually convinced the parts store to return the bad sensor. He got the good part and fixed it for you. He's a good father."

faithfulness

by: breanna rae

Breanna Rae fell down the rabbit hole at the youngest of a grand age, and she has spent her time composing, dancing, painting, sewing, and reciting odd things about crocodiles ever since. She writes poetry when she isn't otherwise occupied, and prefers to not write such nonsense when she is, in fact, quite occupied. Her artwork first displayed inside the halls of a real castle, because of course, and she has studied the great poets of lore including Poe, Plath, and Alice by way of Carroll.

Daydreams barrel into me unexpected
physicality
emotions like a submarine surfacing
in the middle of my parlor—No parlor sounds bombastic
punching through my stomach then
Who knew feelings got so fistic—hollowed out
a melon rind
have to fight a mind that goes rogue
dredges up the past
spread out tangled in
the roots of a willow so serene—

Surreal
I know not what I feel

faithfulness

kindness

by: paul asjes

Paul Asjes was born and raised in Des Moines, Iowa. He spent many summers gardening in Stillwater, Minnesota, and canoeing in the Boundary Waters. He is currently a New York City educator. He has taught math, art, history, reading, and writing. After Colin Witt trained him for his first marathon over a decade ago, Paul loves running. Paul believes that habits help determine our destiny. His book Isaiah's First Winter is a 2023 Mom's Choice Awards® GOLD Award winner.

In the shadow of Mount Merapi, where volcanic mist twined through the narrow lanes of Yogyakarta like threads of batik silk, the Wijaya household held its breath in anticipation. Aminah, heavy with child, lay on a bamboo mat while her husband Budi paced the teak floors, their creaks harmonizing with the distant hum of the factory that dominated their small Javanese town. The night their son was born, the machines in the great factory seemed to purr with unusual gentleness, as if welcoming a new soul into their realm.

They named him Harto—"one who flourishes"—though his mother would often joke that they should have named him "one who tinkers." From his first steps, Harto moved through their modest joglo house like a curious scientist, drawn inexorably to anything that whirred, clicked, or spun. He loved to take apart anything mechanical. Aminah, with her batik artist's soul and hands stained with wax and dye, would watch in wonder as her son dismantled his toys only to reassemble them in new, often surprising configurations. She recognized in him an artist's spirit, though his medium was metal and motion rather than canting and cloth.

Budi, who had worked in the automotive factory since before Harto's birth, carried the scent of metal and oil home with him each evening like familiar sambal. Their small house, nestled in the kampung that surrounded the factory, seemed to pulse with the rhythm of the great machines. During dinner, Harto would sit entranced as his father shared stories over plates of nasi goreng and tempeh, tales of massive engines coming to life, of robots dancing their precise ballet along the assembly line, of the symphony of creation that echoed through the factory halls.

"The machines," Budi would say, his spoon pausing midair as he searched for the right words, "they communicate if we learn to listen, almost as if each one has its own Jiwa." Aminah would smile at this, recognizing in her husband's words the same passion that drove her own art—the ability to see heart and soul in the inanimate, just as she saw stories in the intricate patterns of her batik.

Their home became a sanctuary of creativity, where Aminah's delicate batik paintings of wayang kulit shadows and volcanic landscapes shared wall space with Harto's precisely detailed drawings of engines and gears. The scent of melted wax from Aminah's workshop mingled with the oil and metal from Budi's garage, creating an aroma unique to their family's blend of tradition and technology.

In the cool of evening, when the muezzin's call to prayer floated over the kampung, Budi would spend hours with his son in their small garage, teaching him the basics of mechanics using old motorcycle parts he'd bring home from the factory. These moments were sacred, father and son bound together by grease-stained hands and shared dreams, while the gamelan music from a neighbor's radio provided a gentle soundtrack to their work.

The factory loomed over their lives like a modern-day candi, its massive form silhouetted against the ever-changing tropical sky. To young Harto, it was more than a building—it was a living entity, breathing steam into the air thick with the scent of clove cigarettes and petrichor, its heartbeat marked by the rhythm of assembly lines and stamping presses. He would often stand at his bedroom window during the rainy season, watching the lights of the night flicker like fireflies fallen to earth, while his mother's soft humming of Javanese lullabies drifted up from her batik studio below.

Aminah understood her son's fascination with machines in a way that surprised even Budi. "He sees them as I see my batik," she would say, watching Harto lose himself in repair manuals and technical drawings. "Each part is like a drop of wax, each assembly a complete pattern revealing itself." She encouraged his passion while teaching him that the precision of machinery and the flow of traditional arts were but different expressions of the same creative spirit.

The scent of melted wax and natural dyes from Aminah's workshop would mingle with the metallic tang from Budi's garage projects, creating an aroma that was uniquely their own—a perfume of art and industry that seemed to capture the essence of modern Java. In the afternoons, when the heat pressed down like a heavy blanket, Harto would sit cross-legged on the cool tile floor, watching his mother's canting dance across fabric while listening to his father explain the intricacies of engine timing.

When Harto turned sixteen, the day he had dreamed of finally arrived. Budi proudly presented him with his own set of coveralls, the fabric still stiff with newness, the factory logo emblazoned over the heart. Aminah marked the occasion by creating a special batik piece—an intricate design of interweaving mechanical forms and traditional Javanese patterns, symbolizing the bridge between old and new that their family had become.

But fate—or takdir, as the elders would say—had written a different future in its ledger.

The day of the tsunami began like any other, with Aminah in her studio, carefully applying wax to silk, while Budi and Harto worked their shifts at the factory. The earth shook first—a deep tremor that sent cups rattling in their saucers and birds scattering from the tamarind trees. Then came the water, a wall of destruction that roared in from the Indian Ocean like a thousand angry djinn, destroying everything in its path.

The factory that had been the heart of their world transformed in minutes into a twisted skeleton of steel and sorrow. Harto, who had been outside the main building when the wave struck, clung to a concrete pillar as the waters raged past. When the surge finally receded, leaving behind a landscape of mud and debris, he found himself in a world transformed—the familiar streets of his childhood rendered alien by destruction.

Through the chaos of broken buildings and uprooted trees, Harto searched desperately for his parents, his voice growing hoarse from calling their names into the thick, mud-laden air. The muezzin's call to prayer, usually so punctual, was eerily absent, replaced by the distant wail of emergency vehicles and the closer sounds of human grief.

He found his mother first, in what remained of her studio. Aminah lay amid the ruins of her batik works, protected by the heavy teak table she had ducked beneath. Though injured, she lived—a fact that seemed miraculous in the face of such devastating loss. But Budi, who had been deep within the factory when the wave hit, was never found. Like so many others, he became one with the mud and broken dreams that littered the factory floor.

One afternoon, months after the tsunami, when the factory was starting to slowly rebuild and the workshop was buzzing with the hum of repairs, Harto found himself sitting outside the workshop, absently wiping his hands with a rag. The weight of grief still lingered, but it was no longer the crushing kind—it was a quiet, persistent ache that stayed with him, like the aftertaste of a bitter drink.

He had just finished repairing a motorcycle for a customer who had lost everything in the disaster. The man, an older gentleman with a weathered face and eyes too tired for his age, had brought the bike in, its frame barely holding together after the storm. Harto had spent hours fixing it, not because he expected anything in return, but because the man reminded him of Budi—how a person can be broken but still find a way to move forward.

The elderly customer returned to collect the bike, his steps slow but steady. When he saw the motorcycle gleaming in the late afternoon light, a spark of recognition passed across his face, as if he had just seen a piece of his past returned to him. But instead of the expected gratitude, he stared at it for a long moment, then looked at Harto with a deep sadness in his eyes.

"I can't pay you," the man said quietly, his voice breaking. "I lost everything... my home, my wife, my children." His hands trembled as they gripped the handlebar of the motorcycle, as though holding on to the last fragment of his former life. "I don't have the money to fix this... or to pay for the work you've done. I... I don't even have the strength to care for it properly."

Harto looked at the man, seeing the raw sorrow in his eyes, and something in him shifted. Without a word, he stepped forward, taking the man's hand in his. The gesture was simple, but it spoke volumes—of empathy, of understanding, of a shared pain that connected them both.

"Your bike is ready. No charge," Harto said softly, his voice steady but filled with warmth. "I know what it's like to lose everything."

The man's weathered face crumpled as he fought to hold back tears. His voice was barely a whisper. "But... why? Why would you do this for me?"

Harto gave a small, almost sad smile. "Because someone once showed kindness to my father when he had nothing. And he taught me that kindness isn't a transaction—it's a way of being."

The old man, tears now streaming down his cheeks, nodded slowly. "Your father... he must have been a good man."

"He was," Harto replied quietly. "And I'm trying to be a good son."

With shaking hands, the elderly man climbed onto the motorcycle, and for the first time in months, Harto saw a flicker of hope in his eyes. The man offered a deep, grateful bow before driving off, his motorcycle's engine rumbling with newfound life.

As Harto watched the man disappear down the road, a feeling of peace washed over him, and for the first time since the tsunami, he felt a warmth spreading in his chest—not from the heat of the sun, but from the simple act of kindness that connected their souls. It was as though, in that moment, the act of helping someone else had mended a small part of the brokenness in him.

Later, Aminah, who had seen the interaction from the doorway of the workshop, came over and placed a hand on his shoulder. "Your father would be proud," she said softly, her eyes shining with unshed tears.

Harto smiled, his heart lighter. "Maybe he's watching," he murmured, the words more to himself than to her. "Maybe he's still teaching me, after all."

The sun dipped lower, casting a golden light over the workshop, and for a brief moment, all was still—except for the sound of the wind and the faint, distant hum of the factory. It was the sound of life moving forward, of kindness still enduring in a world that had lost so much.

The months that followed passed in a haze of grief and uncertainty. Harto and Aminah moved into a small room in a relative's house in the hills above the city, their savings barely enough to cover their basic needs. Each morning, Aminah would sit at their window, canting in hand, trying to capture on fabric a world that no longer existed. Her batik works, once filled with the soft beauty of traditional patterns, now held darker undertones—shadows of loss and remembrance woven through familiar motifs.

It was during one of his wanderings through the ruined factory district that Harto discovered the motorcycle, half-buried in mud but somehow not completely destroyed. The sight of it stirred something in him—an echo of his father's voice, speaking of machines with souls. With trembling hands, he began to clear away the debris, revealing more of the damaged vehicle beneath layers of dried mud.

The motorcycle was a Yamaha, one of thousands that had once been assembled in their factory. But this one seemed different—special somehow. Its chrome, though dulled by mud and saltwater, still caught the light like a keris blade. Working on it became Harto's salvation, each cleaned part a small victory against the chaos that had claimed his father.

The arrival of Pak Rahmat, the elderly mechanic who would become Harto's mentor, seemed almost predestined, as if the fates themselves had aligned to bring him into Harto's life. One evening, after hours of frustrating attempts to repair an engine, Harto, feeling defeated, slumped over the workbench. His hands were greasy and tired, his mind clouded with the complexity of the problem. As if answering an unspoken call, an old, familiar voice broke through the silence. "You're looking at it all wrong, anak muda," Pak Rahmat said, standing in the doorway of the workshop, his figure framed by the last light of the setting sun. His face was lined with age, his eyes sharp yet gentle, the kind that had witnessed both devastation and rebirth. He stepped inside, the faint smell of jasmine from his sarong blending with the scent of metal and oil. Pak Rahmat's presence was like that of an ancient storyteller—one who could see the past and future woven together in a single thread.

Harto blinked, surprised. "You're… a mechanic?" he asked, his voice tinged with skepticism. Pak Rahmat chuckled softly, a sound like rustling leaves. “I’ve been a mechanic for longer than you’ve been alive, Harto. But more than that, I’ve learned to listen to the machines. They speak to us, just as the wind speaks to the trees.”The words were simple, but they carried the weight of years spent not only fixing things, but understanding them deeply. Pak Rahmat’s hands moved with precision, as though each gesture was a well-practiced prayer, as if he were part of the machine he was working on, not just a man repairing it. He gestured to the engine Harto had been struggling with. “You must first listen to its heart,” he said, his voice soft but firm. “Before you fix it, understand why it is broken.”

From that moment on, Pak Rahmat’s guidance transformed the workshop into a sanctuary of balance. He taught Harto to blend the ancient with the modern, to respect tradition while embracing progress. “Machines are like people,” Pak Rahmat would often say. “They have spirits, and they remember.” The old man showed Harto how to incorporate the rituals of their ancestors into their work, to offer silent prayers before every repair and to light incense to honor the machinery’s “soul” before disassembling it. While Harto’s hands became more skilled in modern techniques, his heart also grew in understanding the deeper, almost spiritual relationship between man and machine. Together, they found harmony in the workshop, where the hum of engines mingled with the steady rhythm of prayer, and where mechanical solutions were often paired with moments of quiet reflection.

Aminah found renewed purpose in their growing enterprise, her batik skills evolving to create unique designs for motorcycle seats and fairings. Her patterns, incorporating both traditional motifs and mechanical elements, became sought after by riders who wanted their machines to carry something of Java’s soul.

The founding of Wijaya Motors grew from this foundation of family, tradition, and innovation. Their first workshop, built on land cleared of tsunami debris, incorporated elements of traditional Javanese architecture—a joglo roof over modern equipment, bamboo walls framing hydraulic lifts. Every morning, before the first machine was started, incense would be lit and a brief prayer offered—not just for success, but for the wisdom to unite the best of both worlds.

Years later, standing before the new Wijaya Motors headquarters—a building that somehow managed to echo both modern industrial design and traditional Javanese architecture—Harto held his mother’s hand as she unveiled her largest work yet: a massive batik mural depicting their journey from destruction to rebirth. The piece showed mechanical forms emerging from turbulent waves, traditional patterns flowing into technical diagrams, all unified by the warm browns and deep indigos of classical Javanese batik.

Pak Rahmat stood nearby, his aged face bright with pride, while a new generation of workers in batik-trimmed coveralls gathered to witness the moment. The factory that rose from the mud was different from the one of Harto's childhood dreams. Here, tradition and technology worked in harmony, each motorcycle that left their doors carrying something of Aminah's artistry, Budi's passion, and Pak Rahmat's wisdom.

In the quiet moments between shifts, when the machines hummed their eternal songs and the scent of incense mingled with oil and metal, Harto would often find his mother in her studio within the factory, applying wax to fabric with the same precision that he applied to his engines. Together, they had created more than just a company—they had built a bridge between past and future, between craft and industry, between loss and hope.

And in every engine's pulse, every batik pattern, every smooth-running machine, they felt the beating heart of Budi's legacy, living on in the symphony of creation that echoed through their new world—a world where the heart of Java was beginning to dance in harmony with the rhythms of mechanical engines.

joy

by: chad michael cox

Chad Michael Cox is a contract writer for the University of Iowa and the author of the *God of Another World* fantasy book series. His award winning fiction and freelance work has appeared in numerous publications since graduating from the writing and publishing program at Emerson College in Boston, MA, and he is a recipient of the Metro Arts Alliance AWE Champion award for his efforts in supporting and advancing excellence in the work of artists within the community.

Three strands of neon green bubble gum stretched from a broken stick to the thickened sole of Leon's black tennis shoe. He wore the tattered shoe on his left foot. It supported his left leg—the one with varicose veins that caused his calf and ankle to swell whenever he walked. The same leg missing cartilage in the knee which, for that matter, contained little of the once complex bone and ligament structure from his youth. Five surgeries and ninety-three years of life had left him walking with a white beechwood cane which he held like a pistol, assaulting the forest path with each painful step, unsure if he or the pine-laden earth took the greater beating. Him, most likely, since he now sat with the cane in one hand and his leg raised in the air, the gum covered shoe cradled in the hand of another. Some fight. Anyone observing would describe his stalled ascent up the mountain as anything but a heavyweight bout. More like a sparrow pecking at a tin roof: weird and loud and fruitless.

And plenty did watch him on this day ranging from his newest slobbering great-granddaughter, a mere twenty-one days old, to his oldest and most unreasonable son of seventy-eight years, to his younger brother by five years. Rather, some watched. Most passed by on their way to the picnic grounds, but some stayed long enough to show concern, or crack a joke, or simply watch the seemingly feeble attempt to remove a freshly stepped-on piece of bubble gum from his shoe.

Not him. No, they did not watch him. He could no longer tie his shoes let alone reach the substance now impeding his progress. Stuck. Stuck if not for Maelynne, youngest of his four daughters-in-law, and the one who cradled his foot across her lap as she dug the broken stick into and out of each worn down rubber groove. His caretaker. Whether she liked the role or not, she assumed her unspoken responsibility whenever the family gathered. Here they gathered, so she fussed over Leon because of his age and in the absence of his wife, dead these past seven years. He let her fuss for the most part. Arguing with a woman required too much investment, he figured, and he needed whatever energy he had left to reach the promised picnic grounds at the end of this god-forsaken hike.

"You'd think I would notice something so bright sitting on the ground."

She turned to him with a smile, kindly pausing to listen further, but his silence gave her reason to speak, "It could have happened to any one of us."

But it did not happen to any other member of his gathered family, one of whom likely left this ridiculous goop in the parking lot. He could still touch that parking lot if he stretched out his cane. His journey had barely begun before it stalled. No, not anyone else. It happened to him, and he felt foolish. An old fool out for a hike instead of watching black-and-white reruns on a way too small television in an all too lonely community center with too few windows. Indeed, men his age did not step on already-been-chewed bubble gum for many obvious reasons including the fact most of them now lay buried underfoot, so whatever, let his family watch and let Maelynne fuss and let the mountain air fill his still functioning lungs. Better than the alternative.

Leon breathed deeply and looked around at the aspen trees, now fully turned yellow and rustling with a warm breeze. His wife hated aspens. Weeds she called them. He never argued the point because he learned not everything in marriage rhymes with romance, so he kept his passion for the trees a secret and assumed his wife kept secrets of her own, though, he never asked. Another deep breath before turning back to his daughter-in-law. He wondered how many secrets Maelynne carried with her and how they compared with those she could not hide. Those the sun highlighted, several small scars on her forearms, scars she could not remove easily like the shoe she now slipped off Leon's foot, turning it upside down to work at a better angle. She added a pinch of dirt taken from the path, and then some more until the dust removed all evidence of neon life.

"There," she replaced his shoe and tied the laces, "good enough to walk on, at least. The forest will take care of the rest." Maelynne motioned for Thompson, the tallest of Leon's fourteen great-grandsons–who went by Tom whenever his family bothered to acknowledge the shortened name–to help Leon to his feet.

"Thank you, Thompson," Leon spoke his great-grandson's name clearly and loudly and fully at every opportunity, and without apology, because he also gave his own full first name instead of Leo or Lee when called upon to introduce himself. The name suited his parents, so it suited Leon. But if Thompson had reason to complain about his great-grandfather's insistence, well, he kept silent. More than silent. He stayed close, and not simply here along this path. A close relationship. In fact, the boy made it a point to visit Leon every Tuesday afternoon. The two of them played poker with three other men whom Leon considered friends, at least in the sense he knew them, that is to say, they still stood upright and they had cash. The four old men usually gathered at a table near the entrance to the care center where they lived, and then they would wait in awkwardly grumbled, throat-clearing silence until Thompson arrived; and the young con artist typically left the table with more than what he initially brought both in winnings and wisdom. And, well, these men did not play to win, nor did they play to lose. No, it was enough that they played, and they eagerly paid the ante with each dealt hand until, finally, Thompson bid them farewell—despite their predictable complaints they had not played for nearly long enough.

"Your grandmother is up there already," Leon slid his left foot along the path in a casual effort to remove whatever remained of the gift of gum. He also stabbed intentionally at the earth with his cane, reminding nature of the nature of this adventure, assuring himself and Maelynne and Thompson and the rest of his family that he remained at least six feet away from the other side of life. Then, a moment between steps. A quiet memory of his wife and a similar situation. He nodded, "Up there waiting for us like no woman should ever have to wait."

Thompson's grandmother, Sister Sue, as named by her siblings not the church, called Leon her father whenever she had reason to lecture him, and called him daddy whenever she sought to avoid a lecture *from* him. Easily the most dominant personality in the family. So much so, Leon could feel her presence from the womb long before he ever held her in his arms, but he did hold her. He held her often. Until she left him, anyway. Sister Sue married a boy who thought himself a real man. Thought he knew how to treat a woman proper and told Sister Sue as much and more...and more...on and on. Then he left her for another woman, claiming Sister Sue, for her part, did not know how to treat a man, so she and Thompson and Thompson's two younger brothers returned to Leon. But not all of her. Some portion of his daughter stayed behind, and it took years before Leon could feel Sister Sue's presence again. But here on the trail he can feel her, again, and he knows she awaits his arrival. She planned the whole adventure, of course. A celebration of life at the top of a mountain – the same mountain from her youth, the one the family used to visit before broken marriages brought too many kids...kids who spawned grandkids and more...and...the mountain they visited before life and family expanded. Yes, Sister Sue made her plans, and Leon had no option but to attend.

He need only complete a short hike, starting out from the parking lot and finishing at the hidden lake above. Thompson would help him, and Maelynne would care for him, and Sister Sue would have the tables set and the grill started before he arrived at the campsite; and he would make it. He would make it in time to steal the first burger from anyone young enough to think Leon helpless. Young enough to think him an old man. Anyone young enough to think himself man enough to challenge Leon's claim to that blistering, way too hot to savor, breathless-and-gasping first bite. The one that gave him reason to thank his daughter for a job well done even as she apologized for three things she stupidly forgot to bring and another four things she failed to take into account.

"Grandpa Lon! Grandpa Lon!" Rue Melinda ran down the trail with the speed of any respectable eight-year-old who found themselves responsible for the health and well-being of Moose, a stuffed red moose, and Esmeralda, a doll with several tangles and desperately in need of a good grooming. Rue Melinda called him Lon because she still struggled to pronounce Leon's name with an "e" for reasons only a child understands, but mostly, according to her, nobody pronounced the "e" in her name so why should she bother with his name? Leon once attempted to point out the very much spoken "e" in her second name, but quickly succumbed to her greater and altogether elevated reasoning. The old defeated by the young in an unanimous decision. Some fight.

This same undefeated child of sound logic and understanding slid to a dramatic stop before Leon's growing posse of family members, careful not to bump into her grandpa lest he fall to the ground, but not so careful as to avoid the cloud of dust that arose as a result. The dust covered Leon's shoes. He could taste it on his lips and smell it in the air. But these things did not bother the child who continued her proclamation, "There's a lake at the top and daddy says we can fish, but that we have to wait for you and not even until the ceremony ends, so I came back to get you. C'mon, Grandpa Lon!"

The girl with no "e" in her name saw no reason to call him great-great grandpa when he served as her only living grandparent–great or otherwise–and Leon allowed her to call him whatever she wanted. When her other grandpas passed away, he remained. Now he watched as Rue Melinda struggled to take his hand in her own, unsure as to which of her companions, Moose or Esmeralda, should shift over to her other arm. In the end, Leon held both his cane and her Moose, and Moose held Rue.

And Thompson held Leon, and Maelynne still inexplicably held a broken stick with green gum still clinging to the end.

Up ahead, one brother and a sister waited for them to arrive. Sister Sue waited along with her six siblings. More than just Leon's own children gathered, however. Eighteen grandchildren, too, and thirty-three great-grandchildren. Eleven great-great-grandchildren, and one more in the womb. They had all gathered to celebrate Leon. To celebrate his life. To recognize the end of his ever-delayed journey...which he dared not delay further lest he face the wrath of those who loved him, if not so much as they loved food and fishing. So, cane striking forest floor, left foot kicking up whatever dust Rue Melinda did not, Leon took step after determined step.

Until he didn't.

"Grandpa Lon, I'm sad."

But Leon had nothing more to say.

"It's okay to be sad," Maelynne tossed aside the stick.

Walking beside them both, Thompson carried what remained of Leon's life in a ceramic urn, "But Grandpa Lon will always be with us. Especially, here in this place. These aspens always brought him such joy."

love

an interview with

skip asjes

Skip and Linda Asjes have been married and lived in the Des Moines area for over 40 years. They seek to create beauty among people, places, and things wherever they live and travel. They strive to help their children, grandchildren and friends look for beauty in the world around us.

An Interview with Skip Asjes

(The following interview occurred on July 8, 2025.)

Due to impending rain, Skip Asjes sits inside his garage smoking a fresh cigar as my daughter and I approach his family home which boasts a yard filled with a wooden gazebo, clusters of color from well-placed flower beds, and several varieties of tall trees. He has set two additional lawn chairs inside the garage, each with a glass of water next to one of the legs, and invites us to join him as he looks out on nature and the beauty it provides. Before we begin, Skip takes time to engage with my daughter, who is an impromptu guest, and carefully listens to each response. Then, we discuss the dynamics of the interview for a brief minute before I hit record. Skip holds the lapel microphone in one hand, his cigar in the other, as the interview begins...

Chad Cox: When did you first experience love?

Skip Asjes: Well, I think as any kid you first experience love after birth when your parents take care of you. That's, ideally, when you first experience love because we all need to be taken care of and hopefully it's by the parents that birthed you. But looking back, I didn't feel very loved by my parents because of certain dynamics. One was that my mom grew up in a family where my grandfather's family business was the banking business. So, when he would come to visit, he was always in a hurry to get back to the bank to take care of the bank, and I always thought, what the heck? Why don't you take the time to be with your grandkids?

And then my dad's side of the family were in the family business, it was an immigrant business, and so they were very focused on working and building up a business because like my other grandfather, they were trying to provide a living for their, families, but also for people that worked for them...so that's an unusual dynamic, and they knew a lot of people depended on them...the success of their labors. Loving your child or grandchild–I don't think either one of them ever had [or] were given very much about how to do that. Looking back now at my age... so, I'm 67 now, and a lot of these things I've reflected on over the years and [they] weren't very clear to me at the time, but I'd say I felt loved by my grandmother, my mom's mom, because she spent time with us as grandkids reading stories to us.

Isn't that interesting that just taking the time to read a story to a kid makes you feel loved? Then she played games with us, like we'd play Old Maid. My other grandparents just didn't have time. They were too busy working. Looking back now, I'd say I probably never felt seen. My birthday fell [at] the end of April, which is the busiest time of the year in the landscaping business, so my birthday was really just kind of a 'oh-ho-hum, Skip's got another birthday.' But, you know, looking back, I just don't feel like I felt loved. I didn't feel disliked or hated or mistreated. I was cared for. They were good parents [who] did the best they could with what they had. But it wasn't until my wife and I got married [that] I looked back and thought, oh! And I met my wife's mom and dad and I thought, wow, they know a whole lot more about how to love each other…husband and wife and about how to be grandparents. Honestly, that's where I've learned how to be a loving husband, a loving dad, and a loving grandfather. God compensated for my lack of that [while] growing up by providing in-laws who I always felt loved by…and they said it. I just felt loved by my in-laws.

In fact, my wife's mom, she died about, probably 12 years ago, and I've told my wife several times, of all the people that have died in our family. I miss your mom the most because we talked to each other, and I felt loved by her. I never felt the threat that a lot of mothers-in-law feel with [their] sons-in-law.

So, my grandmother on my mom's side… Nobody was really a churchgoer except for my grandma and grandpa [in] western Kansas. I never detected any spiritual life from my grandpa, but [with] my grandma, and [maybe] because she was soft, it felt like life. She gave me a Bible when I was 14 or 15, and it's called The Good News for Modern Man. It had some pictures in it, but not very many, just line drawings, and I distinctly remember reading it out of curiosity. I remember I was 14, probably, or maybe early 15, and this passage stood out to me in…I think it's Matthew 6 [where] Jesus is talking about worrying about how are you going to get enough food and drink, or clothes to wear. Then he says, look at the birds. They don't plant or harvest or store food in barns. If your heavenly father feeds them, aren't you far more valuable to him than they are? And there was another verse that talked about [how] he knew the numbers of hair on my head, and I thought, wow! I distinctly remember thinking, God knows me better than I know myself.

So, it just made sense that God should lead my life. I began to pray every night before I [went] to bed. I can honestly say, probably for the next five [or] six years, I maybe missed just less than six times doing that...so, no matter what kind of condition I was in, when I'd go to sleep, I'd pray, 'Lord, would you forgive me my sins? Would you lead my life?'

I think what happened there was conception. The beginnings of life. The seed of life began right there, and, you know, if you believe that life begins at conception, I'd say I had...I was alive, but it wasn't until my sophomore year of college... I had gotten recruited to be part of a Bible study in my fraternity, and the Christians in the fraternity I lived in, they kind of bugged me because they were pretty goofy and, for some reason, I decided one night on a Saturday night–which is pretty miraculous–I was going to read my Bible. I was going to study. That was it. I was going to study, and it wasn't like I was that big of a studier, or [rather] I didn't have bad grades or anything. But Saturday nights usually were not the night I'd study. I remember feeling kind of wound up trying to study. I thought, well, I'm just going to take some time and read the Bible to calm me down.

Well, there's the hummingbird, by the way. In the top of that tree. [Skip points with his cigar to a nearby tree, inviting us to participate in a moment of beauty which he experienced prior to starting our interview.]

And so, I studied the very first part of John's account of Jesus' life. As I read through it, I got drawn into the narrative and I was in it. I remember getting toward the end, and Jesus...I just felt like he spoke to me and said– he was talking to his friends–and he said: I've loved you, even as the father has loved me. Remain in my love. When you obey my commandments, you remain in my love, just as I obey my father's commandments and remain in his love. I've told you these things [so] that you will be filled with my joy. Yes, your joy will overflow. This is my commandment, love each other in the same way I love you. There's no greater love than to lay down one's life for one's friends. You're my friends. If you do what I command, I [will] no longer call you slaves because the master doesn't confide in his slaves. Now you're my friends, since I've told you everything the father told me.

Well, from about that point on, as I read through the account, I was weeping, thinking that it was really clear that Jesus said, I love you and I'm calling you a friend. It changed my perspective on life, so much. I wanted to run out when I was done and hold that up to all the Christians I knew and say, you've missed it! Here's the most important thing Jesus said, love one another. Somehow that was my sense. That was not present in all the Christians I knew. To love one another, you know, whether that was a fair indictment or not, I don't know, but that was my sense that night.

That was probably in October of 1977, maybe 78...so, a little while ago...a minute ago [anyway]. But there's another passage, one of the early passages I was drawn to–I think I started memorizing some passages because every culture encourages that–[it] was out of Psalms 27. The first part of the psalm is a really meaningful one to me. I started with the first four verses because I could tackle that, but if you go on later in verse ten, [David] says, even if my father and mother abandoned me, the Lord will hold me close. Well, I wasn't abandoned physically by my parents, but I was emotionally. They just didn't know how to connect emotionally with us. My mom...I've never connected with her emotionally, sadly, and I realized that God was saying, even if you feel abandoned by your parents, I'll stick close to you.

So, I've had those unique experiences where God is...when I'm pretty discouraged or distraught...I'll just say, Lord, like, Lord, it hurts. And God will speak to me in a really tender way within a short amount of time just to reassure me that he's listening and paying attention and knowing that he is my father and he loves me.

That probably started to emerge in 1978 [or] 79, and, you know, it's growing. It began to grow at my spiritual birth, or awakening, when I was 19 on that October night. But from that point on, I've just gotten a deeper sense of how much God really loves me, and it really wasn't based on the cross. It was [based] on God...knowing that he had spoken to me in a tender way, just to reassure me that, yeah, you belong to me and I'm not...[knowing] I'm not missing it. Looking back, I think one of the characteristics of feeling loved is being seen. Knowing that you're known, but also that you're delighted in.

I felt like the Lord delighted in me, and one of the ways I experienced that in a really tangible way was when my middle brother contracted pancreatic cancer. He was dying, and I don't know why, but I started just, you know, [like] I kind of do now, I started just walking on the mountain bike trails south of the pool at Ashworth Park below the art center. I remember thinking, oh, this is beautiful. I'd see some really beautiful things whenever I'd take a walk. Well, I grew up in a family that created beauty. I didn't ever consciously think about what role beauty played, but I would do that walk probably 5 or 6 times a week as I kind of agonized over watching my brother die.

So, I would go down to Kansas City and go to chemotherapy with him, once a month, and we'd talk on the phone. We had a pretty contentious relationship growing up. We literally fought with our fists [for] a lot of our growing up, so it was not a warm, fuzzy relationship. My brother was also not a man at peace. He was often volatile, easy to get angry. We just, you know, [it] was like three steps forward, two steps back, kind of a relationship. But the last three years of his life, he started to grow in his relationship with God...he could end up his days at peace with God and the people in his life.

After my brother died, I remember thinking, I still want to walk in the woods. I distinctly remember I felt like the Lord said to me, kind of reached out his hand and said, hey, let's go take a walk together. So, I would go take these walks and it's a part of my spiritual life now to take walks in the woods because, you know, [and] I don't know why I didn't figure this out [earlier], but I am a bona fide plant nerd. I grew up in a nursery family, and we always were looking at plants and trees and shrubs, and so now I'm realizing, well, this is part of how God is, you know, my legacy in my history is to enjoy the beauty of what God's made and also realize how intricate it is because you look at any tree, or anything living, literally, and you realize that the information needed to make that is microscopic, you know. The DNA...all the information to make a huge oak or a huge white pine or a whale or whatever, all the information comes from this little seed and it's like, wow!

I've never really wrestled with [whether] there's a God or not because I also recognized that life is just miraculous–let alone its ability to reproduce itself...let alone its ability to communicate with each other. God has made a system, or a cosmos, that is way more amazing and beyond our ability to describe than [what] we'd ever imagine. I realized God has given me the gift of having eyes to see and appreciate beauty because beauty reminds me that God is real and that he loves me in order to let me experience it; and also loves me enough to give me the ability to create it so that I can share with other's because part of the benefit of beauty is it's also...not only is it healing and therapeutic, but it also gives us the chance to draw people into it. To share it. I mean, it's a lot more fun when you see something that to you is really beautiful and you think, oh, I wish mom were here or dad were here, or maybe your brother, I don't know...just to be able to share it with somebody else and have them blown away by it. It's like it makes our joy complete, and that's part of the story of the good news is that there are people that [can] experience a relationship with Jesus. But because it's beautiful, you don't want to just hold it yourself. It's not as meaningful as it is if you have your friends and loved ones experience it, too.

That just traces back to... There's a passage that my wife and I both memorized before we got married, before we were [even] interested in each other. Isaiah 58, I have no idea why...it's just a random passage, but it says, in the Message, if you get rid of unfair practices...quit blaming victims. Quit gossiping about other people's sins. If you're generous with the hungry, and start giving yourselves to the down and out, your lives will begin to glow in the darkness. Your shadowed lives will be bathed in sunlight. You will always...I will always show you where to go. I'll give you a full life in the emptiest of places. Firm muscles, strong bones. You will be like a well-watered garden, a gurgling spring that never runs dry. You'll use the old rubble of past lives to build anew. Rebuild the foundations from out of your past. You'll be known as those who can fix anything. Restore old ruins. Rebuild and renovate. Make the community livable again...and my take on that now is that God wants to make our communities livable again by restoring everything that's been broken and lies in ruins.

If you look at our culture, it lies in ruins because we're so focused on individualism and wealth [and] success. We have forgotten how to love one another and how to treat our neighbors like ourselves, to love our neighbor, essentially. Well, loving our neighbors is actually kind of a big deal because Jesus said, if we do that then we're accomplishing the law by just loving our neighbors, so it's no small deal.

You know, living here in the neighborhood, I and the people I relate to, I'm just trying to help, whether they're a believer or not, to live in a way that they're able to live beyond themselves [not] just for their own benefit...think about, how can I bless other people in the world that I'm placed in by God? A big part of that is love, so I'm trying to help people and teach them to love your neighbor like yourself, but in tangible ways.

CC: Describe an expression of love that you found particularly meaningful. What made it so impactful?

SA: One of the things that came to my mind when I read that question was, I've worked in an organization that's pretty much a conservative evangelical organization. It's mostly white and they don't know what they don't know. They just don't really know how to relate to the mainstream of what America is, and is becoming...more and more of people that are really different from us. Because I come from a really secular background, I know that people are interested in spiritual things, but they're not interested in joining whatever group we're a part of...and if we're only going to rely on inviting people to come to church with us we're stuck. Most people don't have the time or the interest in doing that, so because of that, I know that if I engage people where they're at, and bring the church to them instead of them to the church, just accept people where they're at...and that I see them...I like them...I like being with them. I can celebrate their stories whether they're a believer or not.

I feel like I'm living out the love of Christ in the same way I experienced it. Interestingly, the only opposition I've gotten to that is from the Christian circles I've been part of most of my life. I had a boss who, you know, I had...not an old...what I call a heritage leader in the organization I work for, and when I talked to him back in 1985 about this idea of people wanting to connect relationally, he just told me...he said, it wasn't the way the gospel spread. He said, that's just humanistic bullshit. And he used that word. I was shocked because I didn't know you could talk that way if you were a Christian. It left me stunned. I told [his] supervisor, and he goes, well, I can't disagree...and I thought, well, welcome to this organization. I was appalled.

But actually, one of the results of that was God spoke to me...several passages where God spoke and encouraged me, saying, don't quit, don't give up. In acts 18, he spoke to Paul in a dream, and then God used that [story] to speak to me directly...where he said, don't give up. Don't be afraid. Nobody's going to set upon you to hurt you. Keep on speaking because there are many people who belong to me in this city. I thought, wow! God...saying, keep on talking. Just keep on saying these things. I've had that happen about a dozen times in the last 40 years where God has said that same thing to me from that passage, you know, [when] you're experiencing opposition. People don't get what we're talking...[what] you're talking about, but just keep doing it because there's lots of people that belong to me and they don't know it yet.

That's the important thing to me. I'm not just trying to influence the people that already know this. I want to connect with the people that don't know this yet. [God was saying] I don't want you to give up talking about what you're talking about because it'll unleash this message...this good news of the kingdom. Lots of people can get in on it–in spite of us–because frankly, most Christians don't care. They just don't care. They're too busy. They're too afraid. They're too, whatever. They just don't care, [but] for some reason, I do...because I was...I was that person...

I didn't come to faith because somebody invited me to go to church. In fact, church has always been a chore for me because it doesn't really relate to the people that have got questions [or] who want to raise their hand [to] say, hey, what about this? It's just...it's not a conducive environment. It's so politically aligned with things that I find repulsive...I just think, wow, who are these people? It's the spiritual family I've been born into, so I'm trying to navigate what it is. What's my role? Why? Why did you put me here, God?

Well, I think part of it is that God said, I want you to keep on speaking, [and] what I find is that it resonates inside of some people. The Holy Spirit is stirring in them similar things, and if I just decided to say, I'm not going to talk about it anymore, they wouldn't hear or be encouraged to continue to pursue what God is revealing to them.

CC: How did you first express love?

SA: My mentor who...he realized the struggle I was in because he was in a similar struggle with the organization and his leadership. We would meet for a black-and-tan about once a month, and he'd share something with me just to try to encourage me. He would listen to my story and commiserate with me. He wouldn't try to fix it. He just let me know, yep, I know what that's like. And he'd pray for me. He said that every time we would end our time together. He'd say, Skip, 'I pray for you and your wife every day' and 'I love you.' I've never forgotten that. Here's a guy, in his 70's at the time, and then he died at 83, even up to the end when I would see him, whether it was when he lived here, or in the city where he died, he and his wife [both], he'd end every get together with love. 'Love you, Skip. Love to your wife. I pray for you guys, every day.' I really miss that because, I mean...I felt very loved by him...so, that's one tangible story.

Well, I had met Jesus, and I think anytime people have a life changing encounter with Jesus, it's the start of a movement of the good news. I had a burden to share with everybody in my fraternity. There were 65 guys in the house. I and another guy shared with everybody in the house over the next year, whatever clumsy way we used to do it. I've had guys come back to me later and say, yeah, I came to Christ because of you sharing with me back then. Most of the guys...my pledge class now are all believers, and it's not me alone because I had another guy who was a believer and we were roommates together...he is the squirrel-iest guy I know. He's so weird. But [then] after I came alive spiritually, I thought, well, maybe he's not such a bad guy, after all. He and I both, together, prayed for and shared with all the guys in our class, and [when] we got together for a reunion a few years ago...all the guys are believers now...and their wives...and their kids. It's like, well, what happened there? I never would have guessed that it began there, when I thought, I need to share this with my fraternity brothers.

[After a few moments of observing the world around him, Skip adds:]

When I would encounter difficulty...like, I had a guy that I really got...[he] had a hard time getting along within my own pledge class. He did some things that were really obnoxious. I remember never being so mad. I would go somewhere by myself and pray, 'God, I would like to just throttle this guy. I'd like to strangle him. I'm so mad.' And then, God would just calm me down and he'd speak to me about something, and I realized, oh, I just need to love him. I need to do what's right toward him, and not want to resort to violence to get even. I realized that God was saying, 'I'll take care of that. You don't need to worry about it.'

CC: How has your understanding of love grown since that first expression?

SA: That's a good question. I hope it's grown. You know, love at its fundamental level is living in a way that it's like [how] it's described in Philippians 2 where it says, even though [Jesus] was...he had all the rights of being God, [but] he didn't count that as anything to live out, and I realized he laid it aside and humbled himself and became human. He didn't seek his welfare. He sought the welfare of the people he lived around. [Paul's] saying that if there's any mind in you at all like that of Christ, then live that way toward other people. Live selflessly. Live a life of selfless sacrifice...and I think I've realized more and more...because of the challenges to that [way of thinking]...that and examples of followers of Jesus, allegedly, who are unable to do that...

They're still living for their own benefit. Whether it's financially, or to get ahead professionally with somebody else... The idea of living a life of sacrificial service is what I think when Jesus said, 'In the way I've loved you, love one another.' Am I willing to live a life of sacrificial service for other people? Am I going to insist on my own way, where I'm entitled to get what I think I need?

A lot of sin is basically...it's an entitlement. People think, well, because I've sacrificed this then I should get this in return. Like, even with God [when] answering my prayers. That's just idolatry. This is going to sound weird, but it never dawned on me that...I think that's what part of the... the whole thing about *do this in remembrance of me*–when we're supposed to remember the Last Supper…of the sharing, the bread and the wine. I think what he's saying is, I want you to remember that this is the life you've been called to…[assuming] you're going to follow me [into a] life of sacrificial service. It won't be fun. It's so counter to the world of, you know, getting for ourselves…taking care of ourselves…not wanting to miss out, or whatever.

So, I probably have grown in realizing that it's…it's the way we live and navigate, and how we approach life among all the people we live around. Am I going to live for myself, or am I going to live in a way where… I read [about] Joseph just recently. Even though he's been betrayed by his brothers, [remember] they tried to murder him…they sell him to some Ishmaelite traders, and then he gets sold to Potiphar and he's put in jail for something he didn't do with Potiphar's wife. He's in jail…completely mistreated, and yet the two guys that get put in there, the baker and the winemaker…[so] they have a dream and they're distressed the next day, and it says [Joseph] noticed they were distressed and said, 'Are you okay?'

That's miraculous. We're so wrapped up in our own lives and our own sense of being aggrieved…we don't even notice when other people are distressed…to ask him the question, are you okay? Can I help you? That was amazing.

CC: Do you find a connection between love and beauty?

SA: Yeah. Beauty to me is a tangible way of experiencing God's love. He gives me the ability and the gift to have eyes to see it and the heart to experience it. Because, as you know, as a creator or creative, there's nothing better than creating something of beauty that other people benefit from. It's like sharing in the nature of God because he made… he's the greatest artist ever…and made the cosmos, which is the most amazing piece of artwork ever…you can't even begin to imagine creating anything on that scale. I'm really grateful that God has given me the eyes to see it and the spirit to respond to it…and recognize it, at least a little bit, for what it is.

Like my friend and his wife. I remember him calling me one time when I was working in the woods, and he said, 'Skip, I've always heard it before, but I've never seen a snowflake.' It was on my daughter's black colored coat. He goes, 'I've looked at it, and I realize everyone's different.' He goes, 'I'm so blown away by the beauty of that.' So, [now] every time I walk by that spot, I pray that God would continue to give my friend and his wife the gift of eyes to see and experience beauty…that he would continue to use them to create it, experience [it], and share it with others.

CC: What are your thoughts on the many definitions of love, ranging from a love for cigars or beauty, to loving a friend or family member?

SA: Well, I just had a recent thought out of Acts 14. I'll have to look that one up...I like how it says it in the Living Translation. So, Paul and Barnabas are in Lystra, Derby. They...let's see. What was it they did? They cast out a demon. Oh, no, [Paul] told the man to stand up and walk. The man jumped to his feet and started walking. When the crowd saw this, they shouted in their local dialect, 'These men are gods in human form.' They set about to try to sacrifice to them. When the Apostles, Barnabas and Paul, heard what was happening, they tore their clothing in dismay and ran out among the people, shouting, 'Friends!' Which is interesting... 'Friends, why are you doing this? Were merely human beings just like you. We've come to bring you the good news that you should turn from these worthless things and turn to the living God who made heaven and earth, the sea and everything in them.'

In the past, [God] permitted all nations to go their own ways, but he never left them without evidence of himself and his goodness. For instance, he sends you rain and good crops, and gives you food and joyful hearts. I think I realize that God wants us to live a life enjoying the things that he has made, but also provides. And it's not just for his favorites, for the people of Israel, or the Christians today. It's for everybody. I think the enjoyment of things in life is part of God's testimony about himself, that he's a good God. He's not a vengeful, hateful god-being. He's a God who wants us to enjoy the good things of life, whether it's good food or connecting with each other as parents and kids or grandkids. This is the path God has set out so that in experiencing that goodness, we may realize God has been really good to me and to us.

I don't think it's unique to just the scriptures or listening to some preacher tell us that God loves us. I think God wants us to experience it in everyday life, and it just happens that I've learned how to appreciate that from a cigar. People have...artists have gone to great labors to make good cigars, and I can appreciate it and think, wow, somebody was really skilled and gifted at doing this. I get to enjoy it, and I also get to enjoy lots of conversations with my friends that we wouldn't have otherwise if we weren't sitting and enjoying a cigar together.

CC: Why do you think we have so many definitions of love and does the definition matter?

SA: Oh, it probably does. I don't get hung up on theological purity, honestly, so I'm going to say, I think there's lots of definitions of love and some of them are more related to pleasure.

A friend of mine thinks that beauty is the main thing, but he refers to the transcendence or transcendental. I'm not sure which one it is because I'm not that educated about it, but apparently in the Garden [of Eden] truth, beauty and goodness were intended to be wrapped and intertwined together, and not separated. It's interesting that the serpent, when he's deceiving Eve, sets out to disentangle truth, beauty and goodness from each other so that he can undermine each of them. I think truth was undermined in a way that made truth be a tool that we could use as a weapon. Goodness could be undermined to make it look [like] people are only good if it's going to be beneficial to them, so it's self-serving. Then beauty can be undermined by singling it out…it becomes perverted…[a] pursuit of pleasure.

Any of those three, if they're not unified with each other, can become an ugly caricature of what it was intended to be. Where beauty is disentangled from truth and goodness, it can easily go down the road of, basically, sensory pleasure; and, as a culture, we're pretty addicted to pleasure. It's become perverted when you talk about beauty. Beauty is way more than that, and has the benefits of being life giving and restorative, causing people to have [better] mental health and emotional health. It's not anything like just the pursuit of physical pleasure.

CC: Which comes first in a relationship: I am loved or I love you?

SA: Yeah, I've thought about that, too. I think I have a different view than I did 30 years ago. I think the idea of meeting somebody and being attracted to them is a supernatural thing, and it may or may not be something that God intends to grow and become something. When it grows and becomes something, you realize there's somebody else in the world that actually thinks about me. That's an amazing realization. To think somebody out there that doesn't have to–I mean, your family has to think about you, or should think about you–but when you meet somebody that you don't really know at all, and you realize, oh, they think about me…and they are the one wanting to make me happy or provide for me. It's like, wow, this is amazing. This is miraculous.

So, sometimes it's based on a physical attraction, but usually it's something more than that. I mean, that might pique our interest, but unless there's something that we see in somebody's eyes, or their smile, or they're taking time to ask a question...and connect to it on a personal level, it doesn't really go much more beyond that.

It's bigger than just physical attraction, but that can be the trigger that starts it. Being created male and female, I think we're made to be attracted to each other. But, yeah, it's kind of a mystery. I think [the Apostle] Paul referred to it as a mystery. I don't know what the sequence is, but I think it's that...as you begin to decide to do that dance together...you begin to realize all the things about love that you never knew before, and I'm still learning things about love 42 years later that I did not realize when we first got married.

CC:To quote the Beatles, do you believe "all we need is love"?

SA: That's a funny question. Well, it doesn't hurt.

I met with a lady who's a friend of my dad's. She was dying of bone cancer. Her cancer came back seven years later, and she was dying of bone cancer, and she wanted to talk to me. She said, 'I have no interest in becoming a Christian, but I want to talk to Skip because he seems kind.' So, I drove down to meet with her and on the way down to KC, I said, 'Lord, I have no idea what to talk to her about.'

I get down there and I'm completely at a loss. But I get there and there's an in-home nurse taking care of her. My dad's friend is in a lot of pain and drugged up. Who knows how much. [She] dismissed the nurse, and the nurse wanted to stick around to hear what I was going to talk about with her. I thought that was kind of rude, [of my dad's friend], but it's her house, her party, whatever. We started to talk, and I said, 'What do you think the good news is?'

That's how I started it. She said, 'Well, I think it's: The love you take is equal to the love you make' That's the back side of Abbey Road by the Beatles...part of their, whatever, it's a long song, a mash up or medley– and I just said, you know, I think I agree.

I had just been reading in Ephesians where...it's in Ephesians 5 and I've been reading it in the Message...[Paul] says, and so I said to Jane, 'What God does, then you do. Oh, watch what God does and then you do it... like children who learn proper behavior from their parents. Mostly what God does is love you. Keep company with him and learn a life of love. Observe how Christ loved us. His love was not cautious but extravagant.

He didn't love in order to get something from us, but to give everything of himself to us. Love like that.'

I said that to her and she goes, 'Wait a minute, what is this?'

'This is a letter that one of the early followers of Jesus wrote to some new followers of Jesus in Ephesus.'

She said, 'I took a cruise once in the Greek Isles and went to Ephesus. I knew it was an important place, but I had no idea why. Now I know.'

And I thought, my gosh, I never have done that before...where I started in Ephesians 5 to talk about the good news, yet that's where we're at. That's what God led me to talk about with her, you know, [do you] realize how much God loves you? He's trying to give everything of himself to you, and that's how he wants us to live. So, in a way, it validates the Beatles song...in the end, the love you take is equal to the love you make.

I think God used the Beatles to talk about love. It wasn't in a pure way, that's for sure, but they really elevated the conversation worldwide about love. I think God was doing something in the midst of a world that was lost because in the middle of the Vietnam War, America was about ready to unravel at the seams...and the Beatles talked about love. That was their main message. I think God was being kind to us.

CC: How does nature inform your expression(s) of love?

SA: A friend and I talked about this. He's another bona fide plant nerd. He has a nursery, or he did, he sold it, but he collects about 25 to 30,000 seeds every year, and then germinates about 15 to 20,000 of them and grows them up to a saleable point. But one of the things [we] realized is we just like the process of raising plants that are going to be a joy to [other] people 75, 100, [and] 150 years down the road. I realized that if you go back into the garden story...[how] God made us in his image, male and female, he made us...he gave us a task or a job...he said, 'I want you to cultivate the garden and be stewards over what I've made.' Wow! Because he made a lot.

I think whenever we're engaged in [or] doing things that affect nature, because [when] cultivating things you're taking what's there and trying to make it even more beautiful–just with the little effort we put into it, a lot of people can enjoy it. I mean, that's what a landscaper does, or an architect or a forester. They're trying to help take what God's made and create environments that are going to be enjoyable to a lot of other people who, frankly, are clueless about the beauty of nature. But if you can be involved in helping bring nature into their everyday world, then they will experience its benefits without even being aware of it.

Like, I landscaped my daughter and son-in-law's house. My grandsons all help me and [my] granddaughter helps me landscape it. My daughter has told me many times, 'I sit on the front porch and I feel like I'm in this garden praying for everything. I just love it. I sit out there and commune with God. So, [basically], I'm communing in this little room you built off the front of our house, and I can smell the smell of the roses and the petunias.' Yeah, that's taking nature and helping bring it into the experience around the people who often don't have the time or the ability to do that.

You know, what's interesting, [and this] may be part of the good news that we've neglected, we have divorced ourselves from the physical world and cosmos thinking they're just not going to be around. We don't need to think about them, because really, God saved us so that we can spend eternity with him. And maybe there's something about being cultivators and tending the garden that we haven't taken very seriously. [But] we should be fulfilling our calling.

In our men's reading group a friend and I were talking about it because he's a doctor in town. He's under a lot of stress, but he landscapes his house and gardens, right. He goes, 'It just feels good to get your hands in the soil and try to raise things from seed.'

I said, 'Yeah, and your garden is lovely [and] I've enjoyed being in your yard for different parties and stuff.' Honestly, I cannot think of anybody in my life that I've known [who] is a gardener, that's not a nice person. They're engaging in something that God made us for. You know, when you talk to farmers, they never struggle with what their purpose and meaning in life is. They don't even question that because they're raising food for everybody. It's like, duh, I'm a conservationist or my land may disappear or wash away. They're always concerned about soil conservation and air quality and nutrients and...

That's what I tell my grandkids. Enjoy nature, whether it's in the Boundary Waters or taking a walk in the woods or gardening in their yard because it'll be a deeper way that they can experience the love of God, and how God's made the cosmos for us to enjoy its immensity. But also its beauty. [I hope] that they don't just go through life in a functional way, looking at people as things...and [that] they realize there's reasons why we live in the world we live in...to experience the beauty of what God has made.

CC: How have you experienced God's love?

SA: Well, I think I've alluded to it or mentioned it already. My mentor is a good example. My wife...being married to my wife. I've learned deep things about love. We enjoy being together. We enjoy...I'm very grateful that we like to do things together: traveling and hiking and experiencing new restaurants. We never dreamed we'd have gone to Europe six times, and to enjoy that together...and see the beauty of other cultures.

There's a beauty in just being companions for 42 years where we're watching out for each other and trying to help each other [learn how] to love our kids and our grandkids and our neighbors together. I think it's the long-term commitment to each other that has helped me to learn and experience things about love that I wouldn't get otherwise. And then seeing the things that came with that, like I said, with her mom and dad, that God used to compensate for the lack of things I got growing up. I'm really grateful for what my wife has brought into my life.

She also loves beauty. She likes to have an environment of beauty in our home, which...more creating things out of textiles and ceramics. But when we have people in our house, she's very cognizant that the atmosphere is part of communicating the good news of the kingdom. I think the good news is something that is inviting. Like an environment. I think people feel the good news way before they understand it. They feel welcomed and comfortable and like they belong before they ever understand what's going on, so creating environments of beauty just elevates that. People think, wow, maybe God is bigger than what I imagined, and [maybe] he's got more to give to life than just saving me for eternity.

I don't know if that makes any sense, but...how we dress...how we present ourselves, our house...we are trying to create environments to reflect the values of the kingdom. It's welcoming. It's welcoming to anyone. It's not just for us. It's what we want our friends and neighbors to experience, too. I'm willing to help any of my neighbors who want advice about their yard, or whatever, I'm willing to help them because I want everybody to be involved in creating beauty in their in their world because I know what it does for me.

I've gotten to know most of my neighbors through being involved with them, whether they ask me for help to come down and just help them, or for them to come help me. Share resources together, tools, expertise... it's part of being a neighbor together.

CC: What is one thing you wish everyone understood about love?

SA: I wish that people could make the shift within the known church from feeling grateful for what God is giving me, to moving towards, 'How can I share this with people in my world?' No longer living just for themselves, but beginning to live in the way that Jesus came, saying in the same way, 'As the father sent me, I'm sending you.' So that they also are drawn into living this selfless, sacrificial life for the benefit of others around us. I see glimpses of that sometimes, but there's an awful lot of fearful actions [taken] out there. The way we are engaging the world around us, basically, it's out of fear. Fear of [not] getting our own.

[The] decisions we make, we make based on pure economics. You know, it may be the right thing to do, but 'I don't want to pay for it,' or 'I'm going to try to save money.' 'I don't care what it does to the people were dismissing or deporting.' 'I just want to save money because we're not going to make it financially if we don't do that,' which ironically, one of the…

We've had a conversation around the 4th of July in our reading group. A really good question was, 'What makes you feel patriotic?' Of course, the answer should have been, well, it's fireworks and waving the flag. And I said, you know, honestly, that doesn't do much for me. I think when I feel most patriotic is when I see our country–that's been blessed by God with so much–freely sharing around the world with other countries and cultures that have so little. It's our obligation. It's our response to God being really generous with us. We can be generous to other nations because God's blessed us. We didn't get it because we're just smarter and harder working than everybody else. It's that God has chosen to give us more than we need, easily, so that we would be a conduit…a blessing to the other nations.

That's what makes me feel patriotic, and that's what grieves me the most about what's going on right now. We've chosen to hunker down and take care of ourselves first. That's so anti good news of the kingdom. It makes me mad. If we're willing to lay down our weapons and, make ourselves vulnerable in order to bless other people, they either accept it or they don't. It kind of goes back to the Abrahamic promise. When, God said through Paul in Galatians that the gospel was announced a long time ago to Abraham saying, 'All the nations of the earth will be blessed through you,' well, the whole promise back then was, I'm going to bless you, but also I'll make you a blessing to this land [which] you don't know anything about. Then I'll bless those who bless you, and I'll curse those who curse you. All the nations of the earth [will] be blessed through you. So, by entering into that risky way of living where you offer yourself as a blessing...and it might just be your friendship, or our friendship...you'll find people that God is stirring, making them alive to himself. God says, I'll bless them, and the blessing is the promised Holy Spirit. It says in Galatians 3, I'm going to invade the lives of people who respond to your willingness to sacrifice to be a blessing...not just live for yourself. Some people won't accept it, and he says, I'll curse those who curse you.

I think it's interesting that when Jesus was being taken to the cross, or experienced opposition, he'd say, 'Lord, forgive them, for they don't know what they're doing.' They have no idea of the ramifications of what they're doing. Again, it's an expression of love, forgiving people that have cursed him and treated him poorly. Ultimately, at the risk of it sounding trite, I think it's intended that love, as it says in I Corinthians 13, it overcomes everything. It's greater than all. It's amazing.

Yeah, hopefully, in talking about this stuff, it stirs people because they think, 'That's what I want to experience' or 'I do experience' or 'I want to share with other people.'

love

But the fruit of the Spirit is love, joy, peace, forbearance, kindness, goodness, faithfulness, gentleness and self-control. Against such things there is no law.

Galatians 5:22-23 NIV

Support Independent Publishing by Purchasing these Titles

The Adow
978-1-7356718-2-6 | Chad Michael Cox

The Adow (5-Ruby Collector's Edition)
978-1-7356718-1-9 | Chad Michael Cox

Inindu
978-1-7356718-5-7 | Chad Michael Cox

Inindu (Favor & Boon Collector's Edition)
978-1-7356718-4-0 | Chad Michael Cox

The Nitch
978-0-9912643-8-4 | Satyrus Jeering

Rumble & Flash
978-0-9912643-5-3 | C. A. Elliott

Shovel and a Prayer
978-1-7356718-0-2 | Todd Partridge

What Grows
978-1-7356718-7-1 | Paul Asjes

NOW AVAILABLE TO ORDER ONLINE AND AT ALL INDEPENDENT BOOKSTORES

IMPRINT TITLES
RUMBLE & FLASH
C.A. ELLIOTT
INDINDU
THE ADOW
what grows

RAE
ASJES
COX
ELLIOTT
FRANCIS
Authors
PARTRIDGE
SEIDLER
JEERING

WWW.YELLOWSUITPUBLISHING.COM